"GOOD WRITING"
IN CROSS-CULTURAL
CONTEXT

SUNY Series,
Literacy, Culture, and Learning: Theory and Practice

Alan C. Purves, editor

"GOOD WRITING"
IN CROSS-CULTURAL
CONTEXT

Xiao-ming Li

State University of New York Press

Published by
State University of New York Press, Albany

For information, address State University of New York Press,
State University Plaza, Albany, NY 12246

Production by Christine M. Lynch
Marketing by Fran Keneston

Library of Congress Cataloging-in-Publication Data

Li, Xiao Ming.
     "Good writing" in cross-cultural context / Xiao-ming Li.
         p.   cm.—(SUNY series, literacy, culture, and learning)
     Includes bibliographical references and index.
     ISBN 0–7914–2679–3 (HC : alk. paper). — ISBN 0–7914–2680–7 (PB :
acid-free)
     1. English language—Rhetoric——Study and teaching—Evaluation.
     2. Chinese language—Rhetoric——Study and teaching—Evaluation.
     3. English language—Grammar, Comparative—Chinese.   4. Chinese
language—Grammar, Comparative—English.   5. English language-
-Rhetoric—Ability testing.   6. Chinese language—Rhetoric—Ability
testing.   7. Intercultural communication.   8. Written communication.
     I. Title.   II. Series.
     PE1404.L5   1996
     808'.042'07—dc20
                                                                                    95-1
                                                                                    CIP

10 9 8 7 6 5 4 3 2 1

CONTENTS

FOREWORD

Xiao-ming Li's study of Chinese and Western teachers of composition continues in a distinguished line of scholarship in rhetoric that spans some thirty years. In the 1960s Robert Kaplan wrote about the differences among the compositions in English of international students. This work led to a series of studies that dealt with what was called "contrastive rhetoric." Many of those studies examined the language and structure of texts written by students writing either in different languages or coming from different language backgrounds and writing in English.

The question that arose in these studies was whether differences in compositions meant differences in the way people thought or simply in the way it was considered proper to express oneself. If it were a matter of thinking, that could lead to speculation concerning the effect of language on the intellect. Some were ready to hop on this idea and the superiority of alphabetic languages.

The studies of the 1980s surrounding the Written Composition Study of the International Association for the Evaluation of Educational Achievement (IEA) elucidated this question by suggesting that national or cultural differences in our structure and style were not dependent on language but on the rhetorical traditions of the society. This hypothesis was supported by an examination of both the compositions of students and by the judgments and comments of teachers who tended to hold common criteria for good writing within their educational system.

Such broad-scale ideas deserve careful and detailed elaboration, and such is the contribution of *"Good Writing" in Cross-Cultural Context*. Li's study of what teachers say about sutdent writing is a meticulous analysis of the operating criteria of expert teachers, those who mold the structure and the style of a whole generation of students. By exploring both the common ground within a culture and the differences between the Chinese and United States cultures, Li has shown how standards are formed and the forms those standards take.

In a postmodern world we see these differences; but within each of the cultures, there is a strong modernist and universalist approach to writing. The two sets of teachers exhibit this tendency. Hence their authority. They are indeed authoring the way another generation of students will write. Some of those students may rebel, but probably few will. Although the teachers may call for individuality of expression, pressure is strong for such individuality to be confined. Such has long been the case and so it will probably remain, but Xiao-ming Li has masterfully turned the mirror on us and forced us to confront ourselves.

Alan C. Purves

PREFACE
A PERSONAL NOTE

I came to America in 1985 from the People's Republic of China to seek more advanced education, yet what I have learned is more than I bargained for. Two advanced degrees from an American educational institution—a master's in Linguistics and a doctorate in Composition Studies and Literature—can hardly tell the epistemological changes I have gone through.

Born the second year after the "New China" was founded under the Chinese Communist Party, I belong to the generation often referred to in China as "born under the red flag and raised under the red flag." The "red flag," however, turned out to be both a blessing and a curse. Having two parents with an impeccable revolutionary past protected me from the many political persecutions and the widespread famine that inflicted the larger population in the early sixties. I also enjoyed the benefit of a socialist society: free education and a guaranteed government job if I did well in school. Things turned on their heads during the ten years of the Cultural Revolution from 1966 to 1976, and my family was torn apart when my parents were targeted as "capitalist agents within the Party" early in the movement. Nine members of the family, except two aging grandparents, were sent to five different places for reeducation.

My education in the early days, like everybody else's in China, was a mixture of Marxism, Maoism, and Confucianism, all of which are based on the deification of an individual whose name is identified with the philosophy. Their doctrines were not to be questioned but studied, learned by heart, followed through in daily life. During the Cultural Revolution the worship of Mao superseded others, Confucius was the fall guy, and Marx pushed to the background. I not only read and memorized the little red book of *Mao's Quotations*, but followed his injunction and joined the Red Guards, smashing street signs and billboards that had any inkling of "feudalistic and bourgeois ideologies," replacing them with such glowing revolutionary names as "Fight Imperialism," "Defend Mao," "Forever Red," et cetera. The fact that my father, the most trusted person in my life, was being incarcerated under the vague accusation of "following the revisionist ideology," though painful, did not stop me from paying allegiance to the Party line. Questioning Mao, the embodiment of ultimate truth and authority, was not only beyond my imagination but too frightening an idea to entertain. I was eventually disqualified from the Red Guards, and later sent to work on a state farm to be reeducated, because of my "problematic" family background. After five years of sweating in the field, I was selected by the local peasants through secret ballot to go to college, despite the fact that I had only a middle-school education. Under the honorable title of "worker-peasant-soldier student," I became a representative of the revolutionary masses that were to take over the superstructure dominated by the bourgeois and revisionist forces—the university.

The Cultural Revolution finally ended when its "great leader" and initiator, Chairman Mao, passed away. My parents' political status was reinstated and the entire family reunited. Like most people in China, grateful only that the long nightmare was over and eager to lay to rest the unhappy memories, I avoided asking the obvious questions: Why did it happen in the first place? Why did the madness have to continue for ten years until the "Great Helmsman" died? Asking "whys" had not been part of my education.

China after Mao went through an exciting political and economic metamorphosis under the new Party patriarch, Deng Xiaoping. The sudden influx of information from outside portrayed the West as a land where one enjoyed total individual freedom and autonomy. Having lived for so long under rigid thought-control and constant political turmoil, the West, particularly America, looked as tempting as a dreamland on earth. The scholarship to study in America came to me as a gift from heaven.

The sense of total freedom lasted for a while after I came to America. No longer did I have to attend weekly political meetings nor monitor what I said in public. The availability of vast information through media and libraries were as attractive as the dazzling display of consumer goods in the supermarket. I devoured books and eagerly made friends, savoring every minute in this democratic heaven. Yet, in time, euphoria was gradually replaced by a nagging sense of desultoriness, whether when shopping for a box of cereal from an array of brand names all looking alike, or, probably felt more acutely, when writing papers for the classes I was attending. In China, the criteria for good writing were as well-stated as the Party line. In America, professors were unwilling to discuss standards, maybe because standards smacked of authority to the American academic just as money once smacked of capitalism in China.

But after I received my papers from the professors with grades and comments, it was clear to me then that standards, though never explicitly discussed, were unmistakably there.

I was considered a good writer in China. Although writing was not a college subject in China and I missed senior high education, my writing teacher in China made enough impact on me in my teen years that I always loved writing. I still remember the "appreciation classes," during which the teacher read aloud to the class a number of the best student papers from the last assignment and analyzed the accomplishments of each selected piece. It was a practice that almost all my Chinese teachers used, and it is still used in most writing classes in China. I remember the pride and joy when my writing was read to the class, and the secret comparison I made with the selected papers when they were read. The climax usually came at the end of the class when the teacher walked down the aisles and handed us our papers with grades and her written comments. Although I often had more or less the same comments— "Well-structured, fluent and expressive use of language. . . "—I cherished the red lines scribbled on my paper, for the teacher was talking to me about my writing, alone. In the reading class, we were expected to understand the content as well as the structure and language of the essays and stories in the textbooks, which were held up as models of good writing. The teacher tirelessly analyzed the content and the formal aspects of each model text. We were told that without the form, the content would have no body, and without the content, the form would have no soul. The favorite story told by one teacher was how a noted poet spent days contemplating whether "push the door" or "knock the door" would best convey the mood of the monk who went to visit his friend under the moonlight. That was why, we were told, "push-knock" meant to weigh one's word, or to deliberate, in Chinese. Through all these direct and indirect instructions, Chinese teachers instilled in me a clear sense of what good writing should be.

In my American classes I soon found myself struggling aimlessly. The problem was not with grades; American professors were much more generous with grades than Chinese professors. The problem was not with grammar or the lexicon, either, supposedly the most daunting aspects of English for a Chinese learner, for although I did have many problems with the linguistic aspect of the language, I could always consult grammar books and dictionaries, and I was used to doing that. It was comments beyond the sentence level in my writing that left me in endless speculation. The instructions were usually kind and encouraging, telling me that I should write "just what you think," and write in my "honest voice." But other comments indicated that to write just what I think and in the way that I felt most comfortable were not good enough. My writing was sometimes "too vague", other times "lacked specifics," and still others "redundant," or I was told that I should "go straight to the point." I was at a loss as to how to be "specific" yet not "redundant," how to avoid "beating around the bush" and to be subtle and suggestive (aren't they the same?), and, more important, what was worth writing. The last was a non-issue in China, since the teachers always assigned the topic. In America I was told to write "whatever you want," yet somehow I knew some topics were more worthy topics than others, but I had no idea what they were.

The confusion continued to dog me when I became a writing instructor myself, reading papers written by students who grew up in a different culture from mine. There was no question to my mind that as a teacher I was setting the standards and wielding enormous power over student writers, yet the criteria for "good writing" were as elusive as ever: What should I say to a piece that "effectively" writes about having fun on a beach and breaking up with her third boyfriend? How to respond to a paper that describes every detail of building a log cabin— from stealing boards from the neighbor's basement to the beer party held in the cabin to celebrate its completion? Should I say "cut it out" or "interesting details"? What grade should I give to a piece that has few realistic details but creates a surreal scene at the top of a mountain: listening to the howling snow mixed with rock and roll blasting from the tape recorder, while gliding effortlessly towards the moon (I was captivated, I had to admit)? Should I say anything at all about a piece that angrily denounces an alcoholic father, who abused the writer's mother and was going to destroy the writer's future because he was too drunk to keep his job and provide for his children's education? How about a piece that calls all men "pigs" and "jerks," probably the way the writer talks in her life? Should I praise her for her courage to assert her own voice or criticize her for using inappropriate language? What is appropriate anyway? Who sets the standards? I realized that I was a standard settee and a setter; I had to decide what standards I should comply with and apply.

Democracy, after all, is still a form of "cracy": rule or government in Greek. The difference, as I see it, is that the standards in America are hidden rather than displayed, and the authority is, as one American instructor put it so well, behind the screen like the Wizard of Oz.

What is interesting is that although Chinese teachers would be more willing to openly admit their power over students than their American counterparts, all parties share the conviction that the standards of good writing, which are meted out through grades and comments, are entirely objective; a good piece of writing is a good piece of writing—pure and simple. My experience in two cultures, however, shows me a different picture: what is "good writing" is a messy and complex issue, anything but pure and simple.

"Who are you? Are you Us or Them?" one reader asked after reviewing my manuscript. My first instinctive response is that I am both, for I have been educated (and have been a good student) in both countries; I have earned my spokeswomanship for both cultures by my extended and firsthand experience with both. Yet, on second thought, I have to say that maybe I am neither. The fact is that I have always been treated as Chinese in America, graciously but with unmistakable distance, after nearly a decade's residence; yet when I visited China for the project I was treated as a visitor, too, showered with flawless hospitality and planned tours that were granted only to "foreign guests." This is an unnerving recognition. Because with that I lose the privilege of an insider, whose allegiance is always beyond question and whose vision is readily shared by others in her country. Yet at the same time it is a unique position, in that I am endowed with a rare double vision, seeing the duality of reality, the truth and untruth in each culture's claim to universal standards.

I would never have imagined a project like this had I stayed in one culture and been exposed to only one set of standards and one brand of thinking. It is the life in both worlds which opened my eyes to the cultural situatedness of "good writing," and it is the pluralistic American culture and the "free-wheeling" discussions in graduate seminars in an American university that broadened my vision to see the deep-seated arbitrariness of all standards and to question the fairness of their enforcement.

I hope, however, that this book will not be read as one-sided promotion of the Chinese way or the American way of seeing. I have lived in both cultures long enough not to romanticize either of them, but my love for both has never diminished by seeing them as they are.

To close, I want to take this opportunity to express my gratitude to people who made this journey over the Pacific possible, and most rewarding.

I want to thank, first of all, Professor Thomas Newkirk from the University of New Hampshire, who convinced me, with his typical sincerity, that my best contribution to the field of Composition Studies in America was to bring in the Chinese perspective instead of discarding it and replacing it with the American. I was acquainted with Professor Joseph Tobin from the University of Hawaii at a critical juncture of the research, first through his work and then in person. He has since steered me in the right direction with his firm and experienced hand. I would also like to thank Professors Patricia Sullivan and Mary Clark for their thoughtful responses to the earlier drafts, and Professor Allen Linden, who, with his extensive knowledge of China and Chinese language from his life-long dedication to the study of Chinese history, is a rare treasure. Most of all I want to thank my friend, Margo Burns, who patiently read all my drafts and was always there to offer help and support.

The journey would have been futile without the support of the writing teachers in both countries who generously gave me their time, wisdom, and, above all, their trust. They are the true experts on this and other issues of education.

As this journey is coming to an end, so has my seven years' education at the University of New Hampshire. I will always remember with gratitude the people who opened their welcoming arms when I first arrived in this new land, and who have since become my mentors and friends: Michael DePorte, Donald Murray, Karl Diller, Rochelle Lieber, Robert Connors, Allen Linden, Mary Clark and many more. They are the ones who keep injecting sanity and humanity into a system under the constant assault of a brutal market economy and narcissistic individualism.

To conclude, I want to thank my husband, Heng Ma, and daughter, Li Ma, who were with me throughout the journey with their unconditional love and cheerful spirit.

The project received financial support from the Central University Research Fund of the University of New Hampshire, and I am grateful for that.

The book is written with teachers in both countries in mind, a balancing feat that demanded more athletic muscles than I possess. The Chinese version, with some revisions, is being published in China. I hope that writing teachers in both countries would benefit from a project like this, and the field of Composition Studies blossom to a garden where flowers of multiculturalism will take root, and flourish.

INTRODUCTION

When asked about the criteria for good writing, Mr. Alloway, Educational Testing Service (ETS) Director of Programs for the Assessment of Writing, responded that "English teachers, though they may have difficulty in giving a verbal description of writing ability that is recognizable to all, can recognize good writing when they see it" (Clark, 134). His response represents the prevailing view, though paradoxical in nature, among writing teachers: what is good writing is an intuitive judgment that almost defies articulation; there is, nevertheless, a muted consensus on what the criteria are. A less popular view is expressed by Knoblauch and Brannon in their book, *Rhetorical Traditions and the Teaching of Writing*, which presents an entirely different, if not opposing, perspective but also discourages further discussion of the issue. Knoblauch and Brannon cite the results of two studies of teachers' evaluations of student writing, one they conducted involving only four participants, and the other by Paul Diederich, which included sixty judges from different professions other than teaching writing, although the reason he chose laymen rather than professionals of writing is not explained. Both studies, Knoblauch and Brannon claim, bear out that, "readers' interactions with texts are complex and multifaceted, based on too many variables to allow any easy definition of the criteria on which 'improvement' should be based" (138). They attribute the chaos to the same cause that led to constant misunderstanding between two comic figures in *Tristram Sandy*: each is much absorbed in his "idiosyncratic perspectives."

Is there a muted consensus or is there nothing but "idiosyncratic perspectives"? The answer does not really matter, because both positions would leave the situation as it is: unquestioned, unexamined, underanalyzed, i.e., accepting the status quo. According to the first position, it is impossible to hold a discussion if a verbal description is hard to come by, and it is unnecessary, since all agree on what it is anyway. If, on the other hand, we adopt the second position, and accept the proposition that criteria for "good writing" or for improvement in student writing are largely a matter of individual idiosyncrasies, there is little point dwelling on the topic either.

Yet to enforce the standard of good writing by supplying feedback on student writing, whether in the form of a summary grade or cautiously phrased commentary, has been a major part of teaching writing, and will continue to be so. Nancy Sommers finds in her research that writing teachers spend an average of at least twenty to forty minutes commenting on an individual student paper (148). In the same chapter of their book, Knoblauch and Brannon state: "We can argue confidently that providing multiple opportunities to write as well as diverse responses to the writing will create conditions conducive to growth" (152). One of the most important functions of the teacher's response to student writing is to offer text-specific advice, to communicate to the student-writer, in subtle or straightforward manner, criteria for good writing. The abandonment of clear articulation and in-depth discussion of teachers' criteria for good writing leaves the basis of this most demanding and probably the most effective part of writing teachers' job unexamined. It is as though an ambitious archer keeps looking for better bows and arrows, but will not bother to find out where the targets are.

This study focuses on the "targets" (what is good writing) rather than the "bows and arrows" (how to teach writing). The goal is not to prescribe what the standards should be, but to describe what have been targeted by instructors who teach writing. Neither does the study intend to formulate a blanket checklist, or two lists, for "good writing." A meaningful discussion of the topic has to take into account the rhetorical situation, the writing task, teacher-student relationship, the educational philosophy of the teacher-evaluator, and other urgencies in any evaluative situation—all the "multifaceted" variables that have discouraged more research on this most important topic from taking place. This can only be accomplished, I believe, by "thick" descriptions of teacher-responders at work in their full contexts.

The study is a "slice of reality," long enough to reach both sides of the Pacific and thick enough to encompass each principal participant's life and work. The purpose is to attempt a comprehensive understanding of the intrinsic arbitrariness and cultural situatedness of the criteria for "good writing." They are arbitrary in that criteria for "good writing" reside not just with the student texts, but, rather, with the teachers who bring in their own values, educational philosophy, aesthetic taste, literary background, and other amorphous factors to their judgment of student texts. Individual idiosyncrasy does not provide a full account either. Teachers' criteria for "good writing" are shaped, transformed, and determined to a large extent by the historical, social, and cultural forces that are beyond an individual's control, and the influence of which no individual can escape. Subjectivity, in other words, is not singular, but collective. And that becomes obvious when the criteria for good writing are examined from a cross-cultural perspective.

CROSS-CULTURAL PERSPECTIVES

To expose the collective subjectivity for "good writing," the study looks at the actual commentary teachers of different cultures deliver, both orally and in writing, when reading and responding to a common set of student papers.

The multiplicity of truth is often brought to light by outsiders, sometimes nonchalantly. In 1838, when most Americans prided themselves on being the chosen few to bear the ark of liberty, and attributed their peaceful prosperity to their founding fathers' legacy of democracy, Alexis de Tocqueville, a young Frenchman, after some intermittent travel in the country, gave an outsider's account. *Democracy in America* became an instant classic.

The reason why outsiders are more perceptive is not that they are more objective. Tocqueville's book reveals just as much his aristocratic upbringing and the effect of the violent French Revolution. Outsiders are no sole possessors of truth; rather, they bring new perspectives to objects that are often too familiar, too much taken for granted by the insiders. A research project that brings together the writing teacher in America and in China, asking them to respond to a common set of student writings, would have the same effect as all good cross-cultural studies: casting multiple illuminations on a familiar object. Which is, in this case, the nature of "good writing."

I choose China certainly because of my familiarity with Chinese language and culture (although that can be an asset as well as a liability), but also because Chinese educational philosophy is as different from America's as one can imagine.

China is remote from America not just geographically but historically and ideologically. It has a literary history of more than three thousand years, developed most of the time independently of Western influence. Ever since the Confucian era, literacy has always been highly valued in China, and the selected intelligentsia were accorded such "frightening halo" (Lu Shun)[1] that in the West only God receives. For centuries, teaching writing was at the core of Chinese education. Natural science, an imported subject, on the other hand, was looked down upon as a bunch of "trivial tricks" (*dian1 cong2 xiao3 ji4*). The Imperial Exam, which began in 587 A.D. in the Sui Dynasty and ended in 1905 when young Emperor Guangxu, urged by his Western-minded private tutor, led the first political reform in China after a series of face-losing defeats at sea, tested solely the candidates' ability to write. The exam was for centuries the only avenue through which one from a humble background could cross the class lines and become a privileged member of the ruling bureaucracy. Therefore, China has well-developed theories and praxes of composition, as well as widely accepted criteria for "good writing." These criteria, of course, have been modified through the years, but, as we will see later, great efforts have been devoted to their continuity.

MULTIVOCAL ETHNOGRAPHY

Most of the ethnographies produced in the field of composition, including Shirley Brice Heath's inspirational research, *Ways with Words*, can be characterized as, to borrow a term from John Van Maanen, "realist tales," because they convey to the reader the sense that "the views put forward are not those of the fieldworker but are rather authentic and representative remark transcribed straight from the horse's mouth" (49). A realist tale invariably adopts a documentary style, recording minute and mundane details, and ends with the researcher's interpretation, with every recorded fact and quotation falling nicely in place, pointing to one inevitable conclusion. There is no indication in such a text that the researcher has carefully culled the facts to support that reading, and, as Maanen points out, "there is simply no space (or perhaps interest) for the underanalyzed or problematic" (53). In a word, the realist model gives the author-researcher the interpretive monopoly under the disguise of objectivity.

Many alternative models are suggested by Maanen. I find, however, Multivocal Ethnography, a new model put forth by anthropologist Joseph Tobin and his colleagues David Wu and Dana Davidson, best serves my project, which is both cross-cultural and ethnographic.

The philosophical underpinning and a detailed account of their method are discussed in their book *Preschool in Three Cultures: Japan, China, and the United States* and further argued in journal papers by Tobin. The salient feature of their approach is twofold: First of all, it successfully combines qualitative and quantitative methods, so it has both the depth of the so-called "naturalistic approach" and the better typicality and representation of the "experimental approach." What is truly unique about their "Multivocal Ethnography," though, is that interpretation is no longer the privilege of the researchers, but a power shared by the researcher and the researched. Although the researchers give their reading of the data, as they should, the local educators and parents are given the same opportunity.

In the study, I followed the procedures set up in the preschool study with some minor modifications. Student papers, instead of videotapes, were used as the primary elicitor of discussion, and the teachers' discussions were carried out both in speaking and writing. The multiperspective, dialogical nature of the preschool project, however, was carefully preserved and followed through, creating what Tobin and his colleagues describe as an ongoing dialogue between insiders and outsiders, between practitioners and researchers, and between people of different cultures (4).

More specifically the study consists of three rounds of discussion: First, four "principal" teachers were selected, two from America and two from China. Each of them was asked to recommend five to six pieces of what they considered the best personal narratives of their classes and explain to the researcher the reasons why they considered those pieces the best by elaborating on their original written comments on the student papers. The discussion as such was between the principal teacher and the researcher on a one-to-one basis.

Second, six pieces were selected out of the pool of recommended papers, and the four principal teachers were asked to comment on all six pieces in the same manner as they did on their own student papers. They were then invited to discuss the comments of other teachers and to explain to other parties their rationale of evaluation when the researcher saw discrepancies in their evaluation. The discussion as such was among the four principal teachers, though they did not meet physically.

Third, four pieces were selected from the six papers and distributed to a wider audience of composition teachers in both countries (thirty teachers in each). The respondents were asked to rank order the papers and explain the criteria behind their ordering. The last round of discussion was, therefore, in the form of a survey, among a larger number of teachers in both countries. The result of data showed how typical the four "key" teachers comments are.

The result of the study, consequently, goes beyond the mere display of the differences and similarities between the criteria for "good writing" in China and the United States, exploring the various informative forces that have fashioned and are still fashioning those criteria.

Throughout the process my role is one of an inquisitive translator and mediator. Some concepts, even when an equivalent could be found in the dictionary of the other language, often carry very different connotations and denotations in the two languages. I asked for elaborate definitions when an abstract concept was evoked in the teachers' comments, concepts like "realism," "honesty," "beauty," and "creativity," as well as simple epithets like "effective," "meaningful," "healthy," and "well-organized." I was a mediator in that I tried to be the "stand-in" for the absent party, asking questions they might ask and raising counterarguments when their views differ, to create a dialogic environment. For instance, when an American teacher talked about linguistic originality in student papers, I brought up a Chinese teacher's view of students as apprentices of language at the stage of imitation, and invited the American teacher to respond to that. Likewise, when the Chinese teacher talked about imitation, I challenged him with the American value of individual perceptions and observations and gave him an opportunity to defend the Chinese view. The meeting of conflicting views was not confrontational, though; the parties involved often readily agreed that there was a good deal of truth in the other's views and modified their own. There lies the difference between a debate and a dialogue: no one has to lose; everyone wins.

THE QUESTION OF REPRESENTATION

The problem of representation became one of the focal points of contention after the completion of the preschool project. Reflecting on the project, Tobin regrets that some participating teachers, after they had seen the result, were critical of the way they were presented in the video: the particular chosen episode made her look more stern than she usually was; juxtaposition of a day-care center from a developing country to one from an affluent, developed country necessarily made the former look shabbier. This is hardly surprising, since selection is power, and decisions as to what to include and exclude are inevitably tainted by the researcher's vision of reality.

To avoid the same pitfall, I took particular caution to ensure fair representation. The following details the major selection decisions.

Four Principal Teachers

The four principal teachers, who were at the core of the study, are from different areas. In China, one teacher was from a so-called key school[2] in Nanjing, a medium-sized city in the south of China, and the other from a school in a rural area, where more than 80 percent of China's one billion people reside. In America, where there is less disparity between the city and the countryside than between communities of different socio-economic make-ups, I chose one teacher from a school located in a university town, which has a mixed population of university professionals and blue-collar workers, and the other from an upscale medium-sized town composed mostly of upper- and middle-class families.

One criterion I followed strenuously was that all teachers had to be strong teachers, teachers who not only teach well but who can articulate their teaching philosophies and are in keeping with new theories and methods in the profession. After talking with at least four teachers in each country, I selected two from each country that I believe possess those qualities.

I cannot claim that these teachers are so typical that their evaluation of student papers accurately reflects the standards of "good writing" in each country—there is no one typical American teacher as there is no one quintessential Chinese teacher. Typicality exists only in approximation, and I believe that I am closer to it by selecting teachers as different from one another as possible. These teachers are typical, though, in the sense that none of them has ever received any education or training abroad; they are products of indigenous education, and they are all excellent teachers according to the local standard, whatever that means.

Six Pieces

The selection of student papers based on the dozens of papers recommended by the principal teachers turned out much more complicated than I thought. I started with a wide search, collecting papers of all kinds, and then narrowed to the personal narrative, a genre widely used in both countries (the research paper, for example, is not taught in China). It is defined as writing that tells a story or a number of events moving over a span of time and is narrated in the first person—supposedly, the writer has experienced the story or the events personally.

I asked teachers in China and America to decide what best represented their students' writing to share with them the power of selection. It was not just a gesture of generosity. One of the most provocative pieces, which elicited strong responses in the discussion, was taken out in the final report because some Chinese respondents complained that its portrayal of rural life in China was "too bleak" and should not be shown to "foreign teachers." Although I regretted its omission, I was obliged to respect their national sensibility.

All principal teachers selected half a dozen or so papers, but when asked to reduce that number to one or two, they resisted. They argued that no one piece could present their idea of "good writing," nor could two pieces do the job, since each piece has its own strengths and weaknesses. They were absolutely right. But I could not possibly include all the papers unless I turned the study into an anthology of student papers—a worthy project, perhaps, but not what I had in mind. I was forced to make the selection on my own. It was a tough negotiation between a manageable number of papers and fair representation. I finally chose, with their consent, six pieces that were comparable in content: from each country one character profile, one reminiscence of earlier life experience, and one piece on resolving internal conflicts.

For the last round of discussion, the tug-of-war between a manageable number and fair representation became even more tense. To have sixty teachers voluntarily read and respond to student papers in the midst of their busy schedules—one thing I learned through working with the four principal teachers is that all writing teachers, no matter where they teach, are survivors of overwork—I had to reduce the number to four. All six papers were so different I was aware that the discussion could take a completely different track depending on which four would go into the final survey. I finally picked the character profile and another on resolving internal conflicts from each country. It is, nevertheless, a carefully meditated arbitrary decision.

Interviews and the Survey

In the interviews and the survey I used open-ended questions instead of a checklist. The result of a check-list survey would be much easier to process, but it assumes that one can know in advance what criteria the teachers are actually applying, which was exactly what I intended to uncover. My interviews with the four principal teachers usually started with questions such as: Why do you choose this piece? Tell me more about why you consider it a good piece? What advice do you give the writer in revision? What improvements do you still want the writer to make? Why do you consider piece A not as good as piece B? What do you see as the strengths and weaknesses of the piece? By asking open-ended questions, I kept the door open to surprises. The same was true with the survey, in which I asked the teachers to comment freely, as long as they would explain the rationale for their ordering of the papers by each paper's strengths and weaknesses.

Certain patterns of evaluation, distinctive of each culture, emerged from the abundance of different voices, despite an ample show of regional difference, philosophical disagreement, as well as individual idiosyncrasies. The result, however, is partly shaped by the many decisions I made during the process: who to talk to, which pieces to include, what information to seek, and what follow-up questions to ask on the spur of the moment. Fortunately, the study does not intend to be definitive. Ethnography, by nature, can only give the reader a thick slice of reality through the representation of the researcher; it is never meant to write the closing chapter.

WRITING THE ETHNOGRAPHY

Finally, the writing of the ethnography. The report is a realistic tale in that I present the story in the temporal and spatial sequences as it happened. But the omniscient narrator that dominates the realistic tales is replaced by a Faulknerian type of narrative as in *As I Lay Dying*: a multitude of tellings of the same story. Different narrators preside at different stages in the telling of the tale of "good writing" in two countries. My own reading, as a researcher and an insider-outsider, comes at the end, not because it is final or conclusive, but as one of many possible readings. I hope such a tale will achieve what successful modern novels can achieve, that is, readers find it necessary to work out their own versions of the story, and they will start to reflect on their own criteria and ways of responding to student papers. Some conventional readers may feel uncomfortable with the lack of closure, focus, confidence, and authority in the report, as I still do with modern novels, but it is the author's intention to give all those privileges to the reader.

The study is not a journey to the "exotic land" of China, nor an exposition on the metaphysical scriptures of the ancient philosophies, nor an introduction to some "inscrutable" Chinese. Although readers may find these along the way, that is not the true purpose of the study. As Marcus and Fischer point out, studies of this kind are moving from "a simple interest in the description of cultural others" to the new phase of "a more balanced purpose of cultural critique which plays off other cultural realities against our own in order to gain a more adequate knowledge of them all" (x).

We can never totally discard culturally imbued lenses when reading and responding to student papers, but we can certainly do better by looking for a while through other lenses. This study is a pair of bifocal glasses, through which we not only have a glimpse of another tradition, another standard for "good writing," another way of reading student texts, but a clearer vision of our own.

CHAPTER 1

Four Teachers and Six Pieces (Part 1)

The first round of discussion was with the four principal teachers: Mr. Wang and Mr. Zhang in China and Jack and Jane in America.[1] With them we have a close look at the life and work of writing teachers in the two countries. Six pieces of student writing were selected to represent their notion of "good writing." The original commentary, both the marginal and the final, on each piece is presented, as are their additional comments at the interviews.

MR. WANG, A "NEO-CONFUCIANIST"

I had a hard time reaching Chinese teachers from America. First I enlisted help from Chinese graduate students studying in American schools, then I sought help from my friends and relatives in China. The result of both was disappointing. One day I received from a friend who must have been tired of my dogged pursuit a copy of "Anthology of Award-winning Student Writings" published in 1989 in China. Leafing through it, I was delighted: there was a teacher's commentary attached to each piece. I immediately wrote to the editor of the anthology, explaining the project and my intent to find cooperating teachers in China. After two months of anxious waiting, I received a long letter from the editor, who turned out to be a high school teacher of writing himself. "After much consideration and delay—I assume you understand why,"[2] the letter begins, "I decided to write you this letter." He continued:

> This project provides an opportunity to introduce Chinese teachers' experience and theories in teaching writing to the West and for us to learn from the West. If successful, it will certainly have a very positive impact on the understanding of the two countries. For this purpose, I would like to cooperate with you wholeheartedly.

The tone of the letter was appropriately formal for such correspondence, yet the writer's enthusiasm was apparent. After a few more letters back and forth, I was confident enough I had found the right partner that I boarded a plane for China.

A few days later I met the editor, Mr. Wang, at his home. Tall and lanky, with his back slightly bent and his complexion wan and wrinkled, he looks much older than his age of forty-nine. He talks slowly, as if contemplating the choice of each word. He always has a cigarette between his fingers, occasionally puffing at it energetically during long pauses in his speech, but letting it burn slowly by itself most of the time. Yet beneath this controlled demeanor is a man of restless energy. Mr. Wang wears a number of impressive hats: vice president of the Society of High School Teachers of Nanjing, president of the Young Teachers' Society (as a mentor figure) in the same city, and a member of the Research Association of the Teaching of Chinese of Jiangsu Province. He is also a classroom teacher, assigned the same teaching load as other teachers.

Through Mr. Wang I was introduced to half a dozen other Chinese teachers, almost all male. The gender gap takes an interesting twist in China. While in America teaching writing is generally considered a female profession, more so at the high-school level than at the college level, in China writing is not a college subject and is a predominantly male profession. Eventually I abandoned my "equal opportunity" plan in China and worked with two male teachers.

It was a homecoming trip after six years away from China. "What a joy to receive a friend from afar!" I was happily surprised that this injunction of Confucius' was still practiced with earnest in China. I was led to Mr. Wang's "humble cottage," invited to his class, introduced to his family and students, and, above all, trusted with his past, stories often painful to recall or to retell.

Mr. Wang's apartment is on the sixth floor of a newly built "teachers' complex," which has neither elevator nor air conditioning. Such complexes have become a familiar sight in Nanjing, the city where Mr. Wang now lives. Located on the northern bank of Yangtze, the longest river in China, Nanjing has a population of more than five million (including the suburban counties), and is considered a medium-sized city in China. It is known as one of the three "oven cities" for its unbearable heat in summer. Since houses in China are owned by the government and rented to the people at a rate lower than the cost of two pounds of pork per month, there is always a great shortage of houses, and owning an apartment is a privilege. In the last decade, because the central government issued favorable policies towards intellectuals, a special fund was allocated by the local government to build more houses for teachers. Mr. Wang was a beneficiary of the new policy and was assigned an apartment four years ago after his family of four had lived in one room for six years. (A plastic sheet separated the room of twenty-two square meters into two sections, one for his wife and him, the other for their two sons.) This new two bedroom apartment was designed to make practical use every inch of floor space, so the "unit," as it is called in China, has no living room. With a couch against one side of the wall, a coffee table in front, and a large photograph of a field lush with bloom-ing tulips hanging on the opposite wall adding an illusionary depth (a gift from a grateful student, I was told later), Mr. Wang has ingeniously turned the narrow hallway into a small yet cozy living room. The hall-way, however, became a narrow pathway only one person could go through at a time. Climbing six floors everyday was an added travail for Mr. Wang's health after a long day at school, and a two bedroom apart-ment without a living room was by no means spacious for three adults (one of his sons is now working in another city), but Mr. Wang is sin-cerely content: "Most people in Nanjing still dream of having an apart-ment like this."

Mr. Wang is well-read in Western literature and philosophy. He likes, in particular, works by French novelists, like Balzac, Maupassant, and Hugo, "because these writers try to be true to reality, and, at the same time, express their own opinions and sentiments." Russian was the most widely taught language in Chinese colleges in the fifties. Mr. Wang learned Russian and read Tolstoy, Chekhov, and Gorky in his college days, but did not like what he calls Tolstoy's lengthy "preaching style." In English literature, his favorites are Shakespeare's *Hamlet* and Whitman's *Leaves of Grass*, as well as short stories by Mark Twain and *Martin Eden* by Jack London. He did not like Dickens's novels much, because "they [Dickens's works] are filled with trivial details, and the mood is too depressing," and he also found it hard to appreciate con-temporary American works, citing three reasons for his disenchantment: tedious plots, confusing structures, and bland language, although he sus-pected the last was the fault of translators. Of all Chinese writers, he admired Lu Shun most for his noble character, his insightful analysis of the so-called Chinese national character, and his relentless fight against the pervasive forces of corruption and hypocrisy.

Mr. Wang did not go out and join the student demonstrations dur-ing "the Tian An Men incidents," but there was no question on which side he stood. Talking about the present political situation in China, he had two comments to offer, one pessimistic—"My generation is not going to see democracy, probably not even my son"—and the other more hopeful—"You watch out, the whole thing is not finished [*mei2 wanr2³*]." He pronounced the last two syllables with the typical Beijing *r*, making them sound both casual and harshly satirical. With some self-deprecation, he commented that the greatest virtue of Chinese intellectuals was their forbearance. "The character of 'forbearance' is very interesting," he observed. "If you look at it carefully, you can see that it actually consists of two characters: a knife and a heart. Forbearance means you can withstand having a knife pointed at your heart. That's very painful, right? But you have to bear it." Often our talks on student papers turned into his deliberation on China's present political situation. He confided that he believed nothing reported in official newspapers (there are no private newspapers in China) "other than the date and the weather forecast." Without reliable sources for news, he had to depend on hearsay, many of which were sheer concoctions. One of the "news" items he related to me was that former Premier Zhao (a leading reformist and former General Secretary of the Chinese Communist Party, removed after the Tian An Men upheaval) just committed suicide according to a Hong Kong newspaper, yet he had no access to any newspaper other than *People's Daily*. I sensed that the frequent meetings of his colleagues and friends in that "living room" are his major source of information. Despite his interest in the West and his years of Marxist and Maoist education, Mr. Wang is a firm believer of Confucianism in his own modified version, holding firmly to the five constant virtues that Confucius advocated in his life: benevolence, righteousness, propriety, knowledge, and sincerity. Sometimes he blames Confucius's influence for some of the educational problems in China, but he believes that many more have been caused by regression from Confucianism.

At the time I went to visit him, Mr. Wang's school had just celebrated its first centennial. The school was founded in 1891 by an American missionary known to the faculty then as Mr. Ferguson, a graduate of Boston University, and it had been managed by American principals until 1926. Times have changed; only the white bell-tower on the top of the school auditorium reminds the visitor of the Western presence on this campus a century ago. The school is now staffed entirely by Chinese teachers and administrators, and attended by Chinese students.

The last day I went to Mr. Wang's school was the day of the middle-school entrance exam. The school gate was heavily guarded by teachers wearing red armbands to keep anxiety-ridden parents out, and I was let in through a side door when they found out who I was—Mr. Wang had notified them ahead of time.

Hundreds of examinees, shut behind the gate, were waiting for the exam. The campus was errily quiet, many students nervously sitting and wandering along the corridors with ivy awnings, some murmuring softly to themselves. They reminded me of those "defining moments" in my own student life. In China, only one out of seven high school graduates can go to college. (The proportion between elementary school and high school can be twice as high, depending on where you live, city or country). The battle to college usually starts from elementary school, and, in some families, as early as the time when an infant starts talking. The first, and maybe the most important, "moment" is the middle-school entrance exam, for admission to a "key" middle school is almost a guaranteed seat in a college classroom. The school where Mr. Wang teaches is the second-best middle school in Nanjing, and the competition to get in is fierce. Mr. Wang attributes this phenomenon, which he describes as "all armies marching to one single-plank bridge," to people's disregard for Confucian teachings: "After the Cultural Revolution the long tradition of pursuing academic excellence was revived," Mr. Wang expounds, with his deliberate pace. "Yet we now have given up everything to prepare students for the college entrance exam. Students have no pastimes, no weekends, and some parents even use financial incentives or physical punishment to keep their children at their books. We are going directly against Confucian teachings." It must be bitterly ironic for him, a Confucian scholar, to see Confucianism, which emerged in a time when the society was torn by violence and greed, and advocated returning to virtue as the only remedy to save humanity from ruin, should be revived at the end of the 20th century by coercion and materialism. He added that Confucius, the saint-scholar who always advocated a rounded character development, specified six arts essential to students, which included horseback riding and archery.[4]

Yet Mr. Wang also criticizes without reservation what he views as the downside of Confucianism. In an article he recently published in a national journal for writing teachers in China, he strongly attacks the Confucian tradition that one should subject all his desires to "the will of the heaven," which translates to the "will of the ruling government" in modern time. He argues that this tradition creates an educational system in China which "gives priority to knowledge, skills, and grades and almost forgets that students are what we teachers are here for." He warns: "We are human beings dealing with human beings. That is at the core of our education. If we forget that basic fact, education has lost its soul." This is hardly revolutionary if said in America, but in China it was like a stone thrown into a serene pond and the splash was loud enough to make him a nationally controversial figure.

Mr. Wang tries to build a more equalitarian relationship with his students. He asked me to attend an after-class activity of his students. The students were putting on plays adapted from O'Henry's short stories, and the whole show was presided over by a student. Mr. Wang appeared on the platform only at the end, briefly introducing O'Henry's life and his impact on literature. The class was not as orderly as I would expect in a normal Chinese class; it was noisy, the students coming in and out and even chatting with one another, yet Mr. Wang did not seem to mind and never interfered. He told me: "In my class I allow students to converse with each other and even disagree with me. I want them to be involved and not just listen to me passively. This is an after-class activity; I let them do what they want." He also tries to create a relaxed political atmosphere is his class. "Students can write literally about anything in my class till the final year, when they begin to prepare for the entrance exam," Mr. Wang said. "I told them, 'Put aside whatever new ideas you have for the time being. You can pick them up again after you get into college.'" While he tries to democratize his class, Mr. Wang is clear-minded about where his class is situated.

Good writing, for Mr. Wang, has to have emotions: "Writing does not have to be very political; it does not even have to have an explicit moral message, but it has to have some kind of feeling, for what one hates and loves expresses one's moral standard."

For Mr. Wang the future of Chinese education lies in "the critical inheritance of Confucianism by borrowing from the West," but Confucianism has to be the foundation as well as the core. Self-perfection is the goal of his life, and his teaching. "I believe writing should be used to understand, improve, and perfect oneself," wrote Mr. Wang in a letter after I returned from China. "In the final analysis, learning to write is not just learning some techniques of writing. It is to enable people to live meaningful lives and to be useful to society." To achieve that goal, he believes that teachers should first of all set an example. His motto is "in peace with poverty, find pleasure in Tao [an1 ping2 le4 tao4]." Tao is translated as "the way of life" in America, yet it means a lot more than that; it can be morality, justice, ideals and principles. Confucius' idea that "inferior men strive for self-interest; great men strive for righteousness" has provided the inner strength for Mr. Wang to bear many political and personal setbacks in his life. He was denounced and publicly humiliated as a "class enemy" in the Cultural Revolution, and was incarcerated for months in an unofficial prison, never told what law he had violated. Yet those painful experiences did not leave in him one ounce of resentment or cynicism.

Mr. Wang is proud to be part of a tradition created by men of high intellect and upright character. "Chinese intellectuals have fine moral traditions that are well exemplified in literature," he says. "Du Fu[5] sighed, after the thatched roof of his dilapidated house was ripped off by the storm, not for his own misery but the multitude, 'If only I had thousands of great mansions to house all the poor in the world, so that everyone will be happy!' Tao Yuanming[6] declares, 'I will never bend [my] head for five *dous*[7] of grain.' They all demonstrated that poverty is not as shameful as the loss of one's moral integrity." He wants his students to be a part of that tradition, which he believes crystallizes the essence of Chinese civilization, although he is aware that he is pointing them to a tortuous road that promises neither fame or fortune.

At the last interview, Mr. Wang stressed again: "China is changing. Old values are being replaced by new, and the old coexists with the new. But one thing is certain: Chinese tradition will survive."

"There was Such an Old Lady" and "Me, Before and After the Exam" are recommended by Mr. Wang as "the best writing I have seen in recent years." He believes that they are typical of the kind of writing that most Chinese teachers would appreciate, and that they also reflect the kind of moral values that should be celebrated in writing.

The author of the first piece, *"There was an Old Lady,"* was his student. The assignment he gave was to write about a good person, a person who had a noble character and was worthy of admiration and emulation. If the students felt that they did not know somebody of such high morality, they could write about an ordinary person, but a morally wicked person was unacceptable. The purpose? "Discover the good, the beautiful, and the real in the students' lives through writing," says Mr. Wang.

THERE WAS AN OLD LADY

There is an image I carry in my mind. Although memory has locked it up for many years, the image remains sharp and clear.

When I was in elementary school, my family lived at the far end of a small lane, quiet and peaceful. Especially in summer, walking in the shade of French parasol trees, one felt restful. Across the road from where we lived was a wall of vermilion color, within which was a small Western-styled house. Often some tiny violet flowers overgrew the wall and spread into the open space in front of our house. I did not know who lived in that small house.

One day after school, I found that I had forgotten to bring my key with me. Having waited outside the home for a while, I was so bored that I put aside the school bag and tried to pick the flowers on the high wall. The wall was so high that I could not reach any flowers and, on falling, sprained my ankle and cried. Pretty soon a small door in that enclosing wall opened and out came an old lady. After so many years, I still remember clearly the first sight of her: medium stature, with a straight back, silver-white hair, and a face cut with deep wrinkles, between the layers of which seeped profound kindness. There was nothing extraordinary about her dress, either. But for some reason, at that time, even at that young age, I sensed something special about her. Now I know it was her disposition. But I did not know what to call it then. The old lady smiled at me affectionately and led me into her small house. Once inside, she applied a medicinal ointment on my ankle and invited me to visit her later on. Returning home, I told my parents that I had met a kindly old lady. Yes, kindness was exactly what I felt from her.

From then on, every time I played in front of the window, whether kicking shuttlecock or jumping rope, the small door would open with a creak and that old lady would kindly invite me to come in and play. What did I play in her house? Nothing—I just told her things about school, about my teachers and my classmates. And she would listen to me quietly, her face radiating ever brightly with smiles. Finally, one day, I could not help but ask her, "Where are the others in your family? Where are your children?"

She was speechless for a while, and then her eyes slowly looked up to the sky above the enclosing wall, saying, as if to herself, "I had a son, but later I lost him."

"What? Lost?" Stricken, I stared at her and said, "My mother always holds my hand tightly whenever we go downtown. You did not hold his hand, did you?" She looked away from me, eyes moist, and then she turned round with her thin back to me—it was still very straight.

At home, I told my parents that the old lady had carelessly lost her son. My parents looked at each other, unable to stifle their laughter. Father told me that the old lady was a veteran revolutionary, thrown into the jail during the Canton Great Revolution. She had joined the Long March, and her son was probably lost during the Long March. My eyes widened: this loving and lonely lady once lived behind bars, and even climbed the snowy mountains and crossed swamps? But why did she look no different from my grandma? A hero in a child's mind is like . . . well, a hero should look close to the sculptures in front of the Monument to the Revolutionary Martyrs. How could she be one of them?

After that when I met her, I became more respectful and reserved, but she acted as if nothing had happened and one day even consulted me about growing more trees in the lane. I then realized that she was responsible for the shade we enjoyed in summer.

Later, the old lady moved away. Before leaving she gave me some flower seeds. Later, a fat man with a big belly moved in, always bragging, "When I joined the revolution. . . ." Later, my family also moved, leaving that wall and that house. Later still, that Western-styled house was demolished.

Ten years or so later, I occasionally went back to that small lane where we used to live. The French parasol trees were still towering and straight. The image of the old lady appeared before me: a modest, affectionate, kind, and ordinary person. She gives me strength and inspiration; she teaches me to be sincere.

Mr. Wang explains that the writer of this piece always had a good grasp of the language, and the paper was excellent when it was first handed in. He made changes in a few places in terms of phrasing and suggested changing the topic from "There Is Such a Person" to the one used now. Other than that, he did not make any substantive changes at all, because he felt the paper was good as it was. The following is his comment on the paper, "There was Such an Old Lady":

Grade: 86. Through direct (what you saw and heard by yourself) and indirect (what your parents told you) description, you quite successfully portray an image of a revolutionary veteran with an admirable character. For the cause of revolution, she sacrificed her son; for the future generations, she planted trees with her own hands. She not only inspired you, but also educated me.

The ninth and tenth paragraphs are somehow rushed. For the rest please read my comments in the margins.

"Grades higher than 85 are good grades in most schools in China," Mr. Wang explains. "Rarely does the teacher deliver 90, and 95 is almost never given, because we do not want students to think that they have reached perfection; we want them to feel that there is still some distance for them to close up."

In the margins, Mr. Wang made four major comments. He underlined the sentence in the fourth paragraph, "She was speechless for a while, and then her eyes slowly looked up to the sky above the enclosing wall . . . ," and commented, "a good detail, accurately depicts the expression of the old lady at that moment." He praised the parts where the narrator says, "You did not hold his hand, did you?" and where she reflects on the image of heroes as the monumental sculptures, for being

"Very realistic." Mr. Wang also likes the contrast created by introducing the fat man into the scene at the end: "This contrast sets off more emphatically the nobility of the old lady." For the last paragraph, he commented, "The fine character of the old lady has already exerted a subtle influence on you."

Asked whether he ever held individual conferences with students, he replied that individual conferences were held "only when the paper is of such bad quality that I did not want to grade it or the paper has some political problems better handled in private." He then gave me an example. Once a student wrote about the border war between China and Vietnam in 1984, which, as declared by the Chinese government, was "a self-defense war to teach the Vietnamese aggressors a lesson." The student, however, expressed doubts in his writing: "Why do we fight a so-called war of self-defense in another country? Is it just or unjust? I don't know. This is an odd [mo4 min2 qi1 miao4 de] war." Mr. Wang called the student to his office and talked to him alone. First, he repeated to the student the official line, "The war is fought in the best interest of our country; every one who loves our country should support it." Then he offered advice of caution: "There are things we don't understand, and if we don't, we don't have to write about them. You are safe with me, for I will not report this to anyone, but if what you have written leaks out, you will be accused of 'smearing the self-defense war' and you can be in serious trouble." Mr. Wang related to the student his own past experience as a cautionary tale: he was incarcerated for nine months during the cultural revolution for having made some off-the-cuff political comments. When he came out, his hair and teeth were both falling out like an old man; he had aged years in those nine months. After the talk, the student never wrote on any "dangerous" topics again. Mr. Wang encourages his students to be critical of trendy thoughts and to expand their horizons outside the classroom, but, to protect the students, he also teaches them to draw a clear line between what can be said in public and what should be kept only to oneself and one's best friends. It is a hard role for Mr. Wang, who views righteousness and honesty, along with others, as the bedrock of his values.

"Me, Before and After the Exam" is from the student anthology that led me to Mr. Wang, who is the chief editor of the anthology. It was written during a composition contest in which the student could choose to write on one of three given topics. Such contests are held frequently in China to simulate the condition of the college entrance exam, and the prize-winning papers are anthologized afterwards to provide models for other students. The other value of composition contests, as Mr. Wang sees it, is to train students to think quickly under pressure, because on such occasions the time is usually limited to two hours, and the topic given on the spot. (What Mr. Wang did not mention is that this form of exam, improvising on a given topic in a restricted time period in a competitive situation, started in 587 A.D., and was then called "Imperial Exams for Civil Services.")

ME, BEFORE AND AFTER THE EXAM

The bell rang for class.

Miss Lee walked into the classroom. When her eyes, obviously searching for someone in the classroom, landed on me, she smiled understandingly. My heart sank, weighing me down so much that I was afraid to look her straight in the eye. How could I misunderstand? There was going to be a preliminary composition test tomorrow, and students coming out of that test would be qualified for the formal composition contest. She hoped that I would represent the class in the preliminary. I felt as if she were saying, "Come on! Win it for our class!" However, my heart was troubled. If only she knew there was another test tomorrow, too.

At dusk, I was strolling along the main street. The setting sun was so beautiful, red as fire, as blood, like a dazzling beauty ready to depart, and whose beauty people were allowed to admire up to the last moment. I walked back and forth along the boulevard, recalling what happened in the class that morning. Tomorrow—there was only one tomorrow; me—there was also only one me. Should I attend the composition preliminary or the ornithology test? I could not answer my own question, and nor could I convince myself either way.

As I strolled on, words of a classmate a few days ago came back. "You, silly you! What's the problem? Of course you'll go to the composition preliminary! Don't you realize that you can get extra credit if you do well in that preliminary? What does a bird contest matter? Besides, Miss Lee will be disappointed if you don't go."

"But I . . ."

I did not know what to say. My classmate was busy, and he ran off, leaving me alone and still undecided. Standing there for a long time, I wanted to cry.

I paced along the endless boulevard. "He is right. If I do not go to the preliminary, Miss Lee will be really disappointed." In order to prepare me for the preliminary, she had tutored me individually, brushing up my skills in writing during her break after the lunch, and borrowing supplementary materials on composition for me. At noon the day before, Miss Lee had called me to her office again. I watched her going through the supplementary materials carefully, her lunch and several bottles of pills pushed aside. Recalling the scene, my heart winced. Disappointing Miss Lee was the last thing I wanted to do.

Maybe my mother was right. As I sauntered along the road, I remembered the long talk between mother and me the night before. Mother didn't agree or disagree with me. She stroked me with a loving hand and said, "A person who can conquer many opponents on a battlefield is a hero. Yet in everyday life, a hero is someone who can conquer himself," quoting the famous saying by the Indian leader Nehru. Mother left me deep in thought. . . .

Looking up, I watched the clouds gradually disappearing beyond the edge of the sky. Yet the setting sun was still so charming, red as blood, as fire, more beautiful in her final glow. A flock of wild ducks flew in front of her, and a minute later, a flock of doves, flapping their joyful wings, flew towards her. What a beautiful sunset! Yes, that beauty belonged to Mother Nature, belonged to all mankind. Let's take care of birds, because they embody the beauty of Nature. Loving birds, taking care of birds was what my heart desired. I said to myself, "Love the birds and do something for the birds. This is what you can give to Nature." I looked up at the setting sun again: happy ducks were charging towards the sun and flying away. I must conquer myself for those happy birds, for the magnificent beauty of the nature before me!
. . . . . .

After I had taken the ornithology test, I returned there. Watching the scene of the setting sun, the ducks were still charging towards the glowing sun and then flying away. No! They were flying faster and more forcefully; they were flying with more beauty and strength! I felt they were singing to me, and my heart opened up to them.

I ran toward the sun, the ducks. I believed I would see my teacher's understanding smile; I believed I would be greeted with the outstretched hands of my classmates; I believed I would hear mother's loving words. Yes, all these would happen! I may have lost something, but what•I had gained was more! The beauty of Nature, the joyful songs of the ducks belonged to me forever!

The person I became was not the same person I was before the tests: free from hesitation, free from conflicts, my heart sings with joy! Toward the setting sun, I fly with the wild ducks.

This piece won a first prize in the contest, and the comments in the anthology are as follows:

This composition is exquisitely designed. The story flashes back as the narrator walks along a street and through the description of her psychological development. The whole piece is, as a result, focused yet natural, warm and touching. Episodes of "classmate's advice," "teacher's tutoring," and "talk with mother" are woven together naturally.

The most outstanding merit of the piece is its repeated brilliant descriptions of the setting sun, which sets the atmosphere of the time, the narrator's character and spirit, and also leads the movement of the narration.

Please read:

The first time when the beautiful sunset is described, it serves as a contrast to the hesitant mood of the narrator, unable to decide which test she should take.

In the second description of the beautiful setting sun, the narrator concentrates on the wild ducks flying high in the clouds and the happy flapping doves to express the narrator's love for nature, which fore-shadows her resolution to conquer self and go to the ornithology test.

At the end, when she comes back to the setting sun for the third time, the narrator is at one with the wild ducks flying towards the sun, her heart singing with joy. As such, she powerfully expresses the theme of the piece: natural beauty cleanses human souls, and mankind should love Mother Nature. The ending triggers the reader's imagi-nation. The three repeated descriptions of the beauty of the setting sun are imbued with strong feeling and sensitivity, which also enable the piece to flow naturally, as if written in one breath, reflecting real life.

Mr. Wang agrees with the evaluation. He concedes, as an after-thought though, that the author somehow overdramatizes the conflict between taking a preliminary composition text and an ornithology test, but he still likes the piece, because, he argues, the writer is dealing with a very real issue for Chinese students, which is how to balance school-work with one's other social responsibilities. In the piece the narrator triumphs over self and makes the right decision. He thinks the piece also deserves high marks for the technical merit praised in the comments.

JACK, A TOUGH-MINDED YANKEE

In his early forties, Jack teaches at a high school in a small university town in New Hampshire. Next-door neighbor to a major state univer-sity, the school seems to gravitate naturally towards higher education. It boasts high SAT scores and upper-level academic courses comparable to university courses. In 1990, 75 percent (the national average is around 50 percent) of the school's graduates went on to colleges or universities. Like a magnet, this public high school attracts students from nearby regions, students whose parents have high aspirations for their children but can not afford the high tuition of a private school.

Jack does not look like a typical Yankee to me at first sight. He is short in stature, and his voice sounds coarse and tired. With well-groomed hair and a corduroy suit, he walks in quick steps and talks in a clipped and fast tempo and with well-chosen diction that conveys precision. He carries an air of formality. Yet deep down he is a man of strong convictions and high work ethics, qualities that remind me of those old tough-minded Yankees who descended from the Puritan tradition. The motto on the wall next to his desk, which is cluttered with student papers and newspaper specimen pages, reads: "Do not pray for an easy life. Pray for a strong person." In his daily swirl of teaching five classes a day, advising the student newspaper, coaching the student drama group, and other administrative duties, Jack still finds time to hold Bible discussions with students from his church once a week during lunch time. Jack has been teaching writing for twenty-three years. As an experienced teacher of writing, he is able to read student papers with the same tempo and precision as he speaks. He seldom falters about his judgment. Usually after he reads the student paper once, he can immediately write or talk eloquently about the strengths and weaknesses of the paper and deliver a grade. With a sharp hunter's eye he is also able to pick up typos and grammatical mistakes in the papers from drafts that have been proofread by several readers. Despite his formality, his relationship with the students is very close and warm. Our talks, held in his classroom, were frequently interrupted by students rushing in to seek his counsel on all kinds of subjects: schedule for drama rehearsals, recovering lost costumes, candidates for the volleyball team, and even some mechanical problems with the light in the school gym. One day, two girls came to request his conspiracy in pulling out a practical joke on a friend of theirs who, they claimed, had betrayed a "serious" vow. Jack winked and agreed.

Jack is a not a Yankee liberal, though; he is a political and social conservative. He loudly regrets that America has lost faith and good values, that students nowadays have little respect for order and tradition, as evidenced by their lack of civility. In our discussion about honesty in writing, Jack could not hide his disgust even though he was speaking in well-modulated tones: "I would like a little polite hypocrisy. I would like to see somebody say to me 'Would you please open the door for me,' rather than have somebody bump into me and then just keep on going." For him, what happened in the sixties started the country on the moral downslide. He described those activists in the sixties as "all these middle-class kids who from my point of view were scorning all the things that had come so easily to them. These spoiled kids who had everything were turning their noses up at it."

Jack grew up in poverty, first in the woods of northern New Hampshire, later in Florida and a succession of seacoast New England towns, as his father, an itinerant automobile mechanic, chased success. The first home he remembers was a one-room cabin with no running water. In school he was laughed at for his "funny speech" and slighted for his "reading problem." "There is nothing either ennobling or picturesque about poverty," he concluded at a young age, and made up his mind to fight his way out of poverty. He became a serious student, and when he graduated from high school, Jack was class president and one of the top students at school. He planned to be a lawyer, yet an unexpected illness jeopardized his plan, and he found himself, instead of at the bar, back in high school, this time as a teacher.

His school years were in the time, as Jack recalls, "before the fall of Archibald MacLeish from the position of a major American poet." Jack still remembers vividly the day when this most respected poet passed away: "That day, the school had a long period of silence. The church bell was tolled its ringing heard all over the town. He was sanctified." For him MacLeish is not just another poet, but a symbol that stands for an era of positive life-affirming literature, and MacLeish's later fall from the literary canon in this country signaled the passing of an era when the line between right and wrong was clear-cut, and hard work and faith were extolled. Then, Jack interposed, some radical changes took place after the turn of the century; the rise of Realism forces the reader to face the seamy side of reality: "Now in Modern art you see bums, hobos, sitting in the doorway of a vacant building with trash all around. Literature portrays people as victims of their circumstances and living in 'the world between the gods.' Now people find Williams's poetry very distasteful, because it is so sappy, so sentimental. So he fell from grace." Jack looked back at the changes with mixed feelings of acceptance and nostalgia: "Now the amount of space to him in American literature is very small. There used to be his very long poem as a must for all school children. Today only a few of his translations from Greek are read." Yet the traditions celebrated in Williams's poems are obviously well alive among the generation who grew up chanting his verses.

During a visit to his home, an elegant two-storied wooden house hidden beside a quiet road, Jack told me with pride that he built the house with his father-in-law seventeen years ago, and that the family had been living there ever since. Entering the house, what immediately caught my eyes was a huge fireplace on one side of the room: its red-brick chimney rising all the way to the ceiling, some wood stacked on one side of the chimney and worn-looking pokers standing in a row on the other side, adding a flavor of antiquity and elegance to an otherwise ordinary living room. In one corner of the living room is a narrow spiral staircase with a wrought iron railing that leads to the second floor, which has an inside balcony overlooking the downstairs and is heated by the huge chimney. Jack's wife came from one of the oldest families in the area and is also a school teacher. One of their daughters has graduated from college and the other is going to college this fall. Their only son is in high school. Jack has come a long way from a one-room cabin in the deep woods.

After a busy day at school, which can tax the strength of the strongest man, Jack still finds energy to write at home. He publishes on a regular basis, usually one article per year in some regional magazine. Jack considers himself a writer and views his relationship with his students as between writers, and his own experience of writing the best teaching guide.

Because the paper he chose seems to have a higher artistic quality than others, I asked Jack if art is what he is teaching. He disagreed:

> The principal purpose of writing is to help people understand something they did not understand before. Art, communication are all secondary. Create something beautiful so it is pleasing to the eye, yet that is the means, not the end. Just like a beautiful painting helps me to understand something, even an abstract design of a rug—in some ways there is an element of understanding. I go to an art gallery and look at the paintings. I am trying to understand what human beings could paint, who painted them, what motivated them, why is that being produced. I understand them better. I just feel they come alive; I understand the way [the painter] looks at the world.

His understanding is obviously not confined to self; writing is a way of expanding one's vision, understanding the surrouding world.

Understanding, knowing the world, is at the core of Jack's perception of the purpose of both writing and reading. The author he is most fond of through most of his life is Charles Dickens, "because his characters are so realistic, but compelling examples of types of people." Thomas Hardy is second on his list of favorite writers," because he helps me probe into the psychological truth of people without them [the characters] even knowing it, " explained Jack. "I mean they even don't know why they are doing what they are doing. That's very valid." When asked whether he is bothered by Dickens's thick and sometimes verbose description, he responded, "I am not saying I love the style so much as I love the characters. I think you can read Dickens despite Dickens' way.

After you have read it ten times, you know the scene and you can go rapidly over it. They [the characters] are so wonderful, you gloss over the rich description." Then I asked him to rate the writers in terms of their style. "Actually I wouldn't put Hemingway at the top, although he is very lean in style," Jack said without any hesitation. "I think I will probably put Steinbeck there. I like him better than Hemingway or Faulkner. He has more poetry in his work than Hemingway, but he's not as obscure as Faulkner." Yet for him, content is far more important than style. "Style, that could get in the way, but when they [books] open up a new world, that's what I want to read," he said. "People can be taught. You can go to a publishing house, they can tell you how to structure a sentence, how a paragraph goes in certain ways, all that stuff, but if the person has nothing to say, all that style stuff is not going to make the book great. I read what I feel I need to know." Right now, Jack feels he needs to know about other ethnic cultures, and he is reading writers from Alice Walker to Amy Tan. Of all the minority writers he has read he admires Toni Morrison most, "Her books make me think in a way I never did before, maybe understanding the black mentality, their way of looking at the world, which I didn't understand very well." Some time ago he read a novel written by a native Chinese writer, and, although he does not remember clearly the title and plot of the novel, he was impressed by the closeness between nature and people in that book, something he feels Americans have just begun to appreciate. He hopes to teach in China in the future to know the ordinary people there and to write about them. His warm feeling towards oriental culture and his eagerness to open his horizons made him an enthusiastic participant in this project.

Jack pulled "Beat Them 'til They're Black and Blue" out of a stack of papers when I asked him to select some pieces that best represent his idea of good writing. The topic was chosen by the student, the form of personal narrative assigned by Jack.

"The writer," Jack says, "is an exceptional student, certainly at the top of the class. She is in the advanced writing class. This piece has been with her for quite a while, and this is the polished piece."

BEAT THEM 'TIL THEY'RE BLACK AND BLUE

My grandfather was a redneck, a poor-born Missouri farmer; never had a full day's rest in all his seventy-two years. A skinny, crooked man, his back was bent forever towards the relentless sun.

Squinting eyes and leathery skin were steadfast reminders of the land and life he inherited from his father.

If he had any love in him, something locked it up behind the hardened grimace he always wore. Sometimes he would slip, and the stern frown etched into his face would lose its conviction. The story's told that when I was born, his first grandchild, he actually hugged my mother, something he never did when she was a child.

Old age seemed to mellow the man. A lifetime of withholding affection ended with me. Unlike his six daughters, I didn't know what it felt like not to be touched by your own father, unless accompanied by the bite of a switch.

I would lie in bed night after night under a wilted cotton sheet waiting for the oppressive Missouri heat to lift. Near my bed was a window which was always open to the sweet-smelling fields. The fire-flies which performed their dazzling dance for me never ceased to amaze my little six-year-old eyes as I waited for the familiar creak of my grandfather climbing the stairs.

He would come into my room and tuck the cotton sheet around my chin. He stayed with me for hours past my bedtime, telling me stories of when he was a little boy. He told me how his family never owned a T.V. or a car. Instead of Saturday morning cartoons, he had Saturday morning chores. After two years in high school, he dropped out because his father needed all the help he could get on the farm. When he was sixteen, his father died, and he became responsible for a family of five. He grew up that year, working in the fields, the only life he knew.

With all the tales that he told, none of them ever included my mom or her sisters. It was like he had willfully erased that part of his life. Some deeper awareness told me to be content with his stories, so I filled in the empty spaces with make-believe stories.

His stories held me until my eyelids became heavy, and his soft Southern drawl lulled me to sleep. Each night before he left me, he kissed my cheek, tickling me with his prickly white stubble. Then he would whisper into my ear:

"Good night, sleep tight,
Don't let the bed bugs bite,
And if they do,
Take your shoe,
And beat them 'til they're black and blue."

With that he would leave me, but the scent of his pipe would linger, protecting me from the bedbugs.

Unknown to me then, each night my mom would come and kiss me good night. She and her father would pass each other in the hall, never touching, never loving. She was a stranger in the house she grew up in.

Jack gave the paper an A and wrote the following comments:

The point of view is reflective first person—from the present looking back. This allows you to understand now what you didn't then. If you want to tell the story from a young child's point of view, the verb tenses would have to change. However, you are commenting on your grandfather in terms of what you understand and saw then, leaving out the understandings you have now. This seems to work very well because it leaves the reader with the job of assessing what it is in him (and in many people), to have a much easier time with unfettered expression of emotion with grandchildren than with children. Your story gives us some clues, but we know there are many factors, different in different cases. The issue isn't so much an explanation of the *reason* anyway. It simply looks at how this behavior affects others—you and your mother.

In the margins, Jack only indicated a few sentences that were unclear to him, but he did not change anything in the paper. He explained: "To put the word in their mouths to me is a violation of the process, which to keep the ownership of their own paper means the words have to be their own."

In the comments at the end and in the margins, Jack continued his dialogue with the writer that started after the student handed in the first draft. Initially Jack thought the beginning—"My grandfather was a redneck, a poor born Missouri Farmer . . ."—was a kind of background, not strong enough to be a good beginning. "Although it was ok," Jack reasoned, "for many noted authors frequently introduce their stories with that, but I felt I was not fascinated by him as a character." He suggested to the writer that the second paragraph be moved to the beginning, "because the mystery of him, what is behind his hardened grimace, may be more interesting as a lead." But in the group discussion, eight of ten students in that group said no, they liked the beginning with the redneck, and the writer herself did not want to change either, so Jack decided that he was not going to impose any change and just stayed with it. In the margin, though, he reiterated, "This para. (the second) is an alternative lead, but your lead is effective as is."

In the final comment, Jack continued his discussion with the writer about the paper's point of view, a discussion started in their conference. The writer said that she was telling the story from the point of view of herself when she was a little child. Jack disagreed, but was unable to convince her. Now with the final draft, Jack put an arrow beside the sentence "Some deeper awareness told me to be content with his stories, so I filled in the empty spaces with make-believe stories," and wrote: "That key sentence justifies the approach you have taken." The approach, as he understood and restated in the final comment, is "reflective first person—from the present looking back." Jack, however, was not suggesting any change, for he considered the point of view that the writer was taking in the paper was quite effective. He was only discussing with the student an issue he considered important for writers. Jack talked more about the piece in the interview:

> In a lean and simple way it shows just enough of the surroundings, as well as a picture of the person. She lets us know that her grandpa is more drawn to the grandchildren than with his own children, but she does not allow us go off at a tangent that might be interesting, but waters it down to a simple story. That's very powerful. She does not rely on phony language. She has a more fluent vocabulary than indicated by this piece, but she is talking about a redneck Missouri farmer, so she picks vocabulary appropriate to the topic as well as to her level. It is also written with a natural style. She has a powerful way of suggesting the whole impact and significance. She does not go into the detail whether she ever beat the bugs, but that is the title. Maybe the title suggests some physical abuse in the family, or her mother was beaten metaphorically. It's subtle and suggestive, and that is excellent.

MR. ZHANG, A LANDLORD'S SON WITH AMBITION

County L, only twenty miles from Nanjing, the city where Mr. Wang lives, is under the administration of the same provincial government, yet the two places seem to belong to two worlds. As the bus left Nanjing for County L, I was struck by the feeling that I had not only left behind human and metallic noises, endless bicycle streams and sundry stores, high-rises and narrow alleys, but was heading to another China, where time flows slowly, if not stagnates. Looking out of the bus window, I saw a peasant woman scrubbing clothes against a slabstone by the river, and an ox was half immersed in the same water. Every inch of field, miles and miles extending infinitely to the horizon, was green with carefully cultivated rice paddies. So peaceful and elemental. I started to wonder if it was the same a thousand years ago.

Mr. Zhang's school was built fifty years ago through the donations of some local gentry and land owners. Although the gentry classes are like historical relics today in China's new political system, and money now comes from entirely different sources, people's attitude towards the school seems to have changed little. A river, winding through the campus, is covered with white lotus flower along the banks. The lotus flower, as lauded in the poem, "grown out of mud, [it] remains unsoiled," is regarded as the symbol of purity and spiritual transcendence. I first met Mr. Zhang at a reception room furnished with chandeliers and shiny brass-edged tables and chairs. The school also boasts a spectacular five-story lab building, an architecture that combines Chinese up-turned eaves and color-glazed tiles with a steel and concrete body. The building was completed in 1987 with about 60 percent of the funding from the government and the rest from the school-run factory. The school is both the pride and hope of the county parents to whom education is the only way their children can leave the land, where hard work yields a living barely above poverty. Education, "reading books" as the local people call it, has been revered and aspired to since the time Mencius preached "Those who labor with their brains govern; those who labor with their muscles are governed." The school has not let the local people down: for the last ten years, it has sent 70 percent of its graduates to colleges and universities each year, a record that puts the school at the top of the best high schools in the province.

Mr. Zhang lives in a small courtyard on campus. It is a typical Chinese peasant house: a two-bedroom, mud-floored bungalow with a big brick stove in the kitchen that burns rice stalks and dried grass. In the front is a small living room, decorated with some scrolls of classic poetry and Chinese brush paintings. Other than an unpainted table and two wooden benches, it is bare of furniture. The back door of the house opens to the "lotus pond," the name for the river that runs through the school. Zhang's wife is a school nurse in a nearby school and his daughter an honor student at the same school where Mr. Zhang teaches. Mr. Zhang's life on the surface looks as unperturbed as the serene "lotus pond" on a sunny day. Mr. Zhang steered clear of any politics, never even alluding, in all the private talks we had, to what happened two years earlier in China's political arena or to corruption running rampant, the two most popular topics on trains and buses and almost everywhere I went in China. Yet it is hard to steer clear of politics in China. Later I found out that his very taciturnity towards politics results from a life much shaped and twisted by politics.

At the age of fifty-one, Mr. Zhang is, except for a recent college graduate, the youngest of an all-male group of teachers of Chinese at the county high school. (This is not at all atypical in China. In Mr.

Wang's office, only one senior teacher out of the ten is female.) The other eight teachers' age range from fifty-two to sixty. One of the reasons why Mr. Zhang is relatively young is because he never went to college. The youngest son of a rich peasant, he was stigmatized as a descendent of "class enemies" from the time he was born, which determined that his future would have little to do with higher education. Yet this young man did not give in to his fate. He worked harder than his classmates, with the belief that top grades would make up for his "faulty" family background. Although he still did not pass the strict screening for college, finally one of his high school teachers, who is now the principal of the school, recognized his superb academic performance and made the unusual decision of hiring him, a high-school graduate and a landlord's son, to teach Chinese in the county high school. Now he is teaching at the same school he graduated from. As a teacher he works with the same zest and determination that took him there. His knowledge of Chinese classic works and his devotion to teaching put him on a good standing among his colleagues. Thin and short, he is a true powerhouse. At a phone call, he took the first morning bus to Nanjing to meet me and the noon bus back to teach in the afternoon. Every paper I sent him was returned with careful and elaborate comments in the margins and at the end.

Although Mr. Zhang was almost ostracized by the system, he never shows any sign of bitterness; rather, he seems even more determined to help his students succeed within the system. In his class, he asks all students to bind their writings into booklets at the end of the semester and choose their own titles for the booklets. I looked through a number of them and was impressed by both their beautifully designed covers and the unique titles. One student names his collection "Morning Dew" and, in black ink, draws in a wood-cut style four upright tree branches with two little buds growing on them and the sun rising halfway behind the trees. Another author, with a fancy for bright colors, uses orange and pink for the background of the cover, on which are the three Chinese characters for "Notes of Searching," and above the characters is a bee, one wing orange and the other pink, surrounded by flowers of assorted colors. The first page of both booklets is the table of contents, written in neat handwriting. Every page of the writing is marked in red ink, its margins filled with comments—they were by Mr. Zhang, in equally neat and careful handwriting. There is no plastic spiral or velo binding; all booklets are threaded or glued together, all bound by hand by their own authors. Evidently the students take great pride in their work and will cherish the booklets as part of their personal archives.

Mr. Zhang is very critical, as most Chinese teachers are, of the present college entrance exam system and mocks it as the modern "imperial examination." He knows all too well that such exams hurt his students in the long run because "they do not write how they really think and feel; they only write what is good for the exam." Yet Mr. Zhang works long hours at school coaching his students to pass that exam. Schizophrenic as it appears, he feels that he has no other choice:

> I love my students. They are country kids and they work very hard. Their lives are much harder than the city kids', so they want to change their lives through education. To change that they have to pass the entrance exam to college, and writing is part of the exam. In the last few years, the writing exam counted for 50 points of the total score (100 points). I told my students, 'If you can score 30 points in writing, you will have a good chance.' If most of my students score under 30 points, it is my responsibility—I have let them down. Personally I do not like the present exam system, yet I have no other choice. I just want to help them to pass the exam.

Education has given him a better life than he was destined to have, and now he is helping his students fight for a better life. The stakes are so high that Mr. Zhang would not do anything to sabotage the chances of his students until the overall environment changes. To help them means to gear his teaching to the entrance exam and to teach the students quick recipes for getting good grades. He provides them with formulas for writing essays, and coaches them to write on safe topics.

He stresses that the content of writing should be healthy and politically correct. When asked the meaning of "healthy and politically correct," Zhang recalled two nationwide discussions on the issue, one in the sixties, the other in the seventies. The first discussion centered around a student composition entitled "Jasmine Flower." The student described with admiration the quiet elegance and serene dignity of the flower, and her teacher gave her an excellent grade. But, when the piece was published in national newspapers for public discussion, it was criticized as expressing "unhealthy bourgeois sentiments" and the teacher was denounced as having failed to measure student writings with correct political standards. In the seventies there was a similar discussion, this time around a student composition with the title, "All Bright?" The student author writes about a beggar he saw around a corner near the movie theater he was going to, which was coincidentally called "All Bright." He then contrasts the "bright" life portrayed on the screen and the dark and sad corner in the real world and concludes, "All is not bright." Since it was in the midst of the Cultural Revolution, the discussion was turned in to one of those "mass denunciation" movements. This piece was denounced as distorting socialist reality with isolated incidents, because it concentrates on one beggar, one dark corner, ignoring the fact that in the New China, the majority of the people are well fed and sheltered, thanks to the leadership of the Chinese Communist Party and the superior socialist system. These discussions certainly taught the entire profession what is "healthy" and "correct," and where the political zoning lies.

Mr. Zhang believes, however, that having a healthy and correct theme is compatible with Chinese literary tradition. In the preface to *The Literary Mind: Elaborations,* the most comprehensive classic of literary criticism in the Song Dynasty (420–589 A.D.), Liu Xie says in effect that "the value of writing lies in the fact that it branches from traditional classics and is an indispensable assistance to government and education." In the Tang Dynasty (618–907), Han Yu, the leader of the literati, further expounded the purpose of writing as disseminating China's moral tradition and being the vehicle of "Tao."

When I asked whether in this tradition there was any place for individual thinking, and whether self-expression was encouraged in his class, he responded:

> We think that writings should have "personality," should come from self and express the author's unique understanding and genuine feelings, yet the "self" in the West is in our view a small "self," and what we are talking about is a big "self." That is, through one's personal observation, discovery, and understanding, the writer should produce works that will contribute to the life and future of the nation and its people, to the health and progress of the society. . . . Self-expression is too easily confused with bourgeois ideas like "self-aggrandizement" and "self-centeredness." It has the danger of turning writing into a means for narrow and selfish interests. If "self-expression" is elevated to the main function of writing, the social function of writing will be weakened, and we run the danger of encouraging the student to wallow in decadent and unhealthy sentiments. We want students to produce writing that can inspire others, and at the same time, enable themselves to think more positively about life, to love life and have more confidence in life.

In his own reading, Mr. Zhang favors the Chinese classics over the modern and the Western. He feels most at home with Chinese classic poetry, and among his favorites are poets from the Tang Dynasty (618–907 A.D.): Li Bai,[8] Du Fu, and Bai Juyi.[9] He regards Li Bai as a Romantic poet and the other two as belonging to the school of Realism. Of contemporary writers, Mr. Zhang is very fond of Ye Shen-tao's works, a contemporary writer and a well-regarded educator, who started from an elementary school teacher. He feels that he can identify himself with the characters in Ye Shen-tao's novels, most of whom are poor intellectuals struggling to avoid sinking to the bottom of the society. He read some Western literature when he was young, but has not read many contemporary works, nor is he very interested in seeking them out, for the few he has read he found boring and hard to comprehend.

"The River in My Hometown" was selected by Mr. Zhang as representing the high quality papers of his students. The topic was picked by the writer and finished in two class periods (forty-five minutes for each period).

THE RIVER IN MY HOMETOWN

Life in childhood is like scattered pearls, bright and shiny, and the river in my hometown is a thread that strings together those pearls of joy and misery, so that I can cherish them forever.

Ever since I can remember, I could see the river flowing in front of me. The river came quietly from the horizon, turning and twisting, making a detour around our small village, and then flowed quietly into the distance. We, as country boys, did not have a playground as city kids did, so the river was our paradise. *When winter was gone and spring came, the ice and snow melting, the earth waking up and seeds sprouting*[10] the willow trees on the river bank showed green, and their branches danced with the spring breeze. The river, which had been lonely all winter, chuckled like silver bells. This was the time when the kids who had huddled in their homes all winter became spirited. Sneaking out of our low-thatched houses, we came to the river bank and climbed up the trees like monkeys, and broke off branches and wove them into crowns. We played the game "catch the bad guy," with those crowns on our heads. When exhausted, we lay on the river bank, looking at the white clouds and the blue sky, while listening to the gurgling river singing. We were even happier when summer came. *Not a thread of clothing hanging on our bodies,* we jumped into the river one after another with loud splashes. We competed in diving or, divided into two groups, fought in the water until our parents came and yelled, "Time to fill your stomach." Dragging and cursing, they forced us back home. In the fall, the river became shallow and pure and one could easily see luxuriant waterweeds and big fish and shrimp underneath. We came in flocks to catch fish in the waterweeds. With good luck, sometimes everyone caught a string of fish to show off to their family. The long faces of the parents would then relax for a while.

However, the river in my hometown did not just flow with the kids' innocence and joy, it flowed with the misery and sorrow of our ancestors. My grandparents worked day and night to fill the stomachs of the whole family. The heavy burden of life bent their backs; *the knife of wind and the sword of frost* carved deep wrinkles into their faces. One midwinter, *in the midst of wind and snow*, Grandma *struggled*[11] to the riverbank with a basket of yams. Half a day passed, and whole family was waiting with *rumbling stomachs* for Grandma and the washed yams for dinner, but we never saw her again. When Grandpa found Grandma at the river, her body was frozen stiff—she was long dead. Whether Grandma drowned or fainted from hunger and then froze to death remained a mystery in my young mind. From then on, the river lost its attraction for me. Only Dad would sit on the river bank, mumbling. Was he trying to call back Grandma's soul or complaining about the *ruthlessness and cruelty* of fate? Oh, the river of my hometown left me a *grievous*[12] elegy.

"Day and night, passing by like the river."[13] Finally, out flowed the blood and tears, and in flowed today's river, full of rosy clouds and happiness. Grandpa did not live long enough to witness that day, and he would never have dreamed that his grandson would now sit behind *clean windows and bright furniture* in the classroom of the County High School, turning the expectations of his ancestors into the dreams of tomorrow.

The following are Mr. Zhang's comments:

Grade: 90. This is lyrical prose, with the beauty of poetry. The story takes unexpected twists and moves fast in time and space, yet, with the river in your hometown as a thread, you managed to link the materials together, which demonstrates your ability to control materials. In terms of expression, you organically combine emotional expression with the narration, creating a piece that not only has a strong flavor of rural life, but is permeated with your love for your hometown and people. It draws from both the colloquial and the classic poetry and proverbs, and the language is simple and natural, demonstrating good literary grace

It is a narration written with strong emotions. The last paragraph, though, is not as specific as the foregoing ones, therefore the final effusion of emotion is not well founded.

Mr. Zhang explained that he often responds to the student papers in one of three ways: one, written comments; two, oral comments in the student's presence; three, an individual talk with the student, in which the student is directed to revise the paper by him/herself. The first method is used more often than the other two. The student-author of "The River in my Hometown" wanted to send the paper to the school student publication after the paper was finished and graded, so he approached Mr. Zhang for advice on revision and Mr. Zhang talked with him individually. The final draft shows a number of major changes compared with the first. The beginning of the third paragraph was crossed out: "My hometown is a tiny village in the country. The diligent country folks there were simple and honest, but also very ignorant; they believed in the power of heaven and ghosts." Also crossed out was the second sentence in the fourth paragraph: "For years and for generations, people on both sides of the river lived in low and yellow mud cottages. Here the earth was yellow, the cottages were yellow, so were people's complexion and even their teeth." The whole concluding paragraph was rewritten, which originally was: "I love the small river in my hometown. On its sand river bed, on the branches of the willow trees along the riverside, in the cattail clumps and the clear water are my childhood dreams and joy, as well as the sweat and blood of my ancestors." The episodes of Grandma's death and Dad's lonely mumbling at the bank were added.

The revision is based on an understanding of the theme of the paper, which, according to Mr. Zhang, is the contrast between the past and the present, and between the lives of the generations, to underline the great changes in people's lives brought by socialism. The parts about "yellow faces" and their superstitious beliefs are, therefore, not relevant to the theme, and the change of the conclusion has the effect of highlighting how the memory of the past influences the author's life now, which echoes back to the beginning statement, "I can cherish them forever." The added episodes, he explains, further enhance the theme. The paper was later accepted and published by the student literary publication of the school.

JANE, A CONVERTED LIBERAL

Jane, an American high-school teacher in her early forties, is the mother of two young adopted sons. She teaches in a high school in a sizable, affluent town, inhabited mostly by upper-middle-class business people and professionals. It is more than half an hour's drive from where Jack teaches. While Jack's town has a single main street without traffic lights and is crowded mostly with small restaurants and snack shops catering to cash-strapped college students, the town where Jane teaches is criss-crossed with car-jammed streets lined with antique stores and elegant restaurants. In the town is a private school known as the best in the entire United States, and, as a result, the richest and the best students are attracted to that school after they have finished junior high in Jane's school. "I don't get to teach the best students," Jane lamented.

All my meetings with Jane took place in her home. Of medium height, with blond hair curling and hanging loosely over her shoulders, she looks much younger than her age of forty-something. Her words are enunciated with such a crisp edge that they came through clearly in replay even when my tape recorder was dragging on low batteries during the recording. Whether it is a natural gift or a result of teaching English for nearly two decades, I cannot tell. Occasionally Jane dresses elaborately in flowing stylish clothes with slightly puffed sleeves and low-cut in the front, but more often she is in a shirt and jeans, which nicely set off her slender figure. Our talks are frequently broken with laughter, giggles, and sidetracks to our favorite topic, parenting.

The house was built by her husband, who is a school counselor on weekdays and a construction worker during weekends. The house is different from any houses I have ever seen in the area. It is connected to the garage with a vestibule, opening to the outside with a round door consisting of two half circles, closely resembling the moon-shaped doors in Southern Chinese gardens. When a four-door closet in the living room is pulled opened, Jane's hidden study is revealed: a computer on a shelf-like desk and piles of paper spilling from the shelf onto the floor. When the doors of the closet are closed, the clutter is hidden from view, leaving only a grand piano and an oriental rug in the center. The house is spotlessly clean in spite of two young boys running around, one of them a toddler who leaves a trail of toys behind him.

Jane lives a fast-paced life. To catch her I had to call her before six in the morning before she took off for work, dropping the two boys with a baby-sitter on the way. Upon entering the house she snatches the phone that has been ringing off the hook and cradles it between her shoulder and chin, talking to, and, at the same time, appeasing the two most active boys in the world. One is determined to cry his heart out until he is allowed to play with the real screwdriver; the other quietly but with the same determination reaches for the water boiling for cocoa on the burner. Jane catches the quiet saboteur in time with the phone still hanging from her shoulder. Our conversation usually does not start rolling smoothly until both boys fall asleep.

Jane says from the beginning that she feels very uncomfortable commenting on papers whose authors she does not know, still less to grade them. Only after I urge her to read the papers as drafts and conference with me as if I were the author does she finally accept that role. As for the grade, I soon realized that it is not a useful index anyway since the value of the grade varies widely from one teacher to another. Jane characteristically begins her comments with "I like" or "I love," and her criticisms are never phrased as passing judgment but more as tentative advice: "I might ask her to . . ." or "I would like to see more . . ." She handles students papers like a caring mother cradling a delicate baby.

Jane grew up in a very intellectual family; both of her parents are well educated. Because of such role models at home, Jane had always been a good student: "I bought into the educational system because my parents bought into it and I respected them very much. I respect them both intellectually. I never thought I could match them, so I struggled. Grades were very important to me." In the sixties, she could not understand why her friends were so discontent, and felt embarrassed being unable to align herself with their cause. After college, Jane was single for the next fourteen years, during which she began another educational process; this time, in the real world. She traveled to Europe and met so many different people there that it did not take long for her to discover what an inadequate education she had received in school. "These were very sophisticated and capable people. They lived a simple lifestyle but had a rich spiritual life. It was very exciting. Yet I was not taught to think; I was taught to take in what they [the teachers] understood and to express it back to them in their terms." At the age of twenty-two, Jane became an English teacher, but she did not want her students to be what she used to be, an echoing machine without a mind of its own. She wanted them each to be a unique individual who could think on his or her own. She became more idealistic at the age of forty than she had been at twenty.

Jane's idealism, however, is put to test daily at school, where democracy is more an ideal than reality. Students confessed to her, with no qualms, their secret formula that would guarantee good grades in most classes: "We just pretend to understand something and use a little bit of the instructor's language and ramble on about something but not too much." "Is that lying?" she asked. "Yes," the students were frank about how they coped with the system. Jane is convinced that both the system and the students stand to lose if the system produces "winners" who have no language of their own. "They speak in such cliches and such slang," said Jane, very upset. "They speak all the time in cliches and slang, that you can almost take everything that the students say during the course of the day and find that nothing is new. There is no new thought. They are afraid to appear intellectual, for they feel it is phony to be philosophical or to try on more sophisticated language."

Teaching writing is her way of fighting back. Reflecting on her teaching, she says:

> As a writing teacher, I really take an extreme stand. I want my students to be more sophisticated than they are used to, to try on lots of different things. I throw problems at them and ask them to learn new ways to read and write. I want them to dig inside, to discover life for themselves and use language to express their thinking and feelings. Otherwise you only get what you want. Now I am getting papers I am pleasantly surprised. I believe they can learn.

Writing for her first happens at a very personal level. Jane loves Don Murray's definition of writing and quotes it several times, although quoting is something she rarely does: "All writing is autobiography." On the function of writing, she ruminates:

> All writing is persuasive. A narration persuades people to see their experience, see their perspective. One of the purposes of writing is to clear things for themselves. First and foremost is to relate to themselves, to see clearly how much they know or don't know, how much they feel or don't feel, and then to say something to people. Once they make the breakthrough that writing takes them deeper and helps them see things more clearly, then they can begin to choose purposes for it. The question I throw at them is, "So what?" "What is your purpose?" "Do you want me to laugh or want me to feel?" Writing should have significance.

Jane believes writing class is a place for experimentation, not perfecting what one already knows, and the students are graded according to how successfully they have discovered new language, new ideas, or something new about themselves. "When I am grading, I am looking at the writer. Very often my A- is to indicate something was done very well, but not all is right." One student summarizes in the journal her learning experience in Jane's class: "I have learned a lot about myself." That's exactly what Jane wants to accomplish.

Asked to name her favorite authors, Jane pauses for a while and then says, "Faulkner comes to mind. He blows the language and grammar apart." She was using *The Sound and the Fury* as the text in her literature class at the time of our interviews. But she refuses to call it teaching: "I am not teaching. I am not saying a word. They love it and get it." She also names Toni Morrison for her book *Song of Solomon* as one of her favorite authors. "Good writing," she generalizes, "has to have an impact. It has to move me in some way, whether it moves me to be disgusted, moves me to fall in love with the writer. It has to move me into some kind of emotion." Good writing, for Jane, starts at a personal level and connects with the reader at a very personal level, too.

As she is engrossed tirelessly in turning her students to themselves, Jane has transformed herself: "I think I am more liberal now. I think if I were shot back to the sixties, I would be a different person."

Jane has strong religious beliefs. She was raised to believe in God and perceives herself being "still very Christian," even though she does not go to church regularly now. And she believes that that liberalism does not weaken her faith in God. Religion for her is not taken on blind faith; it is a way of life, "A very positive view of life," she told me. But she is careful not to bring her personal beliefs into students' school life, since the last thing she wants from her students is to "think all like me."

The two untitled pieces, one about a friend's suicide and the other about the author's summer vacation, were both selected by Jane from her own student writings. The subject matters were, as often happens in her class, generated from talks in workshops and individual conferences in and after classes.

UNTITLED 1

The world is still going to revolve, the calendar pages are still going to turn, and life will still go on as usual for most everybody. That's why it makes me so mad that you committed suicide. What could you have hoped to accomplish? Yes, your problems are solved now, but ours have just begun. You've not only left your problems behind, but also an entire lifetime of love from family and friends and me. But you will never feel any love now, because you're dead! How could you do this to me? I'm sick and tired of taking other peoples' feelings into consideration! How about me? I have feelings, too! You were my best friend, and now you've left me to sink and swim on my own! I am so angry and confused. Why? Why did you do that? Life would have gotten better. I know it would have.

I remember the day we met like it was yesterday. Both of us so alone, scared and nervous. But we met and talked. It was both of our first time at camp, so we didn't know anybody else, remember? We became immediate friends. It was the funniest week of my life. We shared our life stories, laughed and cried when the week ended. Fortunately, you lived a mere half-hour from my house. Remember all the late phone calls, telling about my first boyfriend, first kisses, and your parents' divorce. We were always there for each other when we were needed. But where are you now? I really need you now, and where are you? You aren't here where I need you the most, and I don't think that I can forgive you for that.

Soon after we met, you told me that I was your best friend. I was so glad! I had never had a best friend before, and I felt the same about you. We always told each other everything. Why was this any different?

Maybe it was me. I thought about it a lot. Maybe you tried to tell me and I wasn't listening. But you left no explanation. Just a heart-wrenching puzzle for the people who cared about you to piece together.

But now who am I going to talk to, listen to? Who can I count on? Not you, because you're gone. You're gone, and it hurts so much. I really need you now. I loved you like a sister. We called each other every night, filling hours with dreams, fantasies and hopes. But who can I call now? I have new dreams, new hopes, ones that you will never know about. There are so many things that I want to tell you, but your ears will never hear me.

Of all the jumbled emotions I feel, angry, confused and hurt, I just need you to know that I miss you. I hope that wherever you are, that you can lend an ear to listen to me. I want you to watch me grow, as my anger disappears. Your life is over, at such a young age of fifteen, yet mine has just begun. I just want you to know that until we meet again, I love you, friend.

Jane's written comments are very simple, for she is so much involved in the entire process of the composition that she does not need to say much at the end, when the product is finished: "A- This is a *moving* piece, _____ (name of the student). You found what it was you had to say."

The student did not find out what she had to say all by herself. It started as a piece described by Jane as "a poor attempt at formal essay, a piece that says nothing," and also one in which "authority is missing— she didn't say anything that we don't know." The first draft begins with: "You know, every day I hear people complaining that their life 'sucks,' because their parents won't let them do something." Then the author went on to write about a movie, her aunt's attempt to take her life when drunk, and some general discussion of the threat of nuclear war and drugs. In the middle of all these she mentioned, "I read about suicides all the time, and a person I know committed suicide, so I know the effects."

The piece ended with some general advice about life: "Put down the weapons and shake hands. Try life without drugs for a change. "This is it. No curtain calls."

The piece was obviously poorly focused, and the writer did not really know what she wanted to say. The only place in the piece where the writer showed personal interest in the topic was the part on her friend's suicide, so at the conference Jane asked the student what really happened with her friend. The student became emotional and told Jane about their relationship and the impact of the death on her. Jane then wrote beside those disturbing lines in the paper, "Use this experience to *show* the effect on others!" But the student resisted. In the next draft, instead of writing about her friend, she wrote about a film:

> I've recently watched a movie called "Permanent Vacation." It's about a gifted high school boy who committed suicide because of his scholastic and social pressures. The movie focused on the effects of the suicide on his friends and family. It really put things into perspective for me.

Then she goes on with four more paragraphs on life in general, and the ending comes back to the suicide issue: "Suicide is not the way to go. Live for yourself and life will become quite a bit better."

Jane asks her students to keep a journal to reflect on the their writing process. The writer, in this case, realized that her writing was hitting a wall, so she wrote in her journal to Jane:

> My subject was suicide. It was supposed to be a story, but it came out more as a lecture. With topics like suicide I couldn't find a way to have somebody die by suicide without giving a message that is strong enough to say don't do it . . . . I felt that I made a few good points about the topic, but it just didn't seem strong enough or story like.

Jane was less concerned about the genre, whether it was a story or an essay; she wanted the student to connect writing with real feelings and to use writing to find out what she really thought about the topic. So she had another conference with the student to see what was significant enough to be developed in the piece. Again the student mentioned that she had been unhappy after the death of her friend. Jane suggested that maybe she should confront her feelings and write about them. A few days later, the student came back with a piece charged with heartbreaking emotions and "a strong message" (Jane's words). Jane suggested some corrections to spelling and sentence structure and let the student decide if she wanted to do more about it. This time the student wrote in her journal:

On this piece, there wasn't much I could change because this wasn't a "story." It was a letter to a friend. I did change a few lines as I realized new things while I wrote. But mostly I just copied it down. I am glad you told me to try again with the suicide piece, because *even though it's very personal, its come to help me realize a few things I hadn't known before.* (emphasis added by Jane)

Jane was pleased, not so much with the final product as with the discovery the student had made through writing. She sees authority in this piece, which was missing in the previous drafts. "Authority comes from the fact that she had a personal experience, she has strong emotions, and she expresses them. It is not cliche-ish; she says something no one else can say," said Jane, her eyes sparkling with delight. "Writing in this case has become meaningful, because it is used to deal with life, and that is what writing is for." Jane underlined the last line and wrote beside it, "Good for you!"

UNTITLED 2

With the arrival of summer my thoughts would turn towards the unkempt lakehouse with the shaggy lawn and ancient appliances. It wasn't spectacular to look at, but it was a refuge from the modern, fast-paced world.

I spent the last two to three weeks of every childhood summer at the family summer house in the Adirondack Mountains of New York. It was located on a small, peaceful lake in a hamlet. There weren't enough people to call it a town.

Although there was a lack of children to play with, my brother and I were never bored. We would spend hours on the rocks surrounding the lake catching crayfish. We would use these creatures for bait on our long trips in the rowboat. Occasionally one of us would catch a walleye or a trout, but for the most part we arrived home with a bucket full of rock bass. We proceeded to skin these fish, and my mother would fry the minuscule fillets for appetizers.

I remember well carrying my father's golf club bag down the first two holes of the course across the street. At this point the five-dollar bill waiting at the ninth hole would seem like so little, and I would abandon my father to scamper through the woods, looking for golf balls. I would emerge covered with dirt and with burs tangled in my hair, but I would be smiling as I proudly unloaded my pockets and made a mountain of golf balls for my father.

In the heat of the day I would happily plunge into the cold mountain lake, and Eric and I would play many games. Late afternoons were usually spent climbing trees and exploring the woods where it was cool.

As each day came to a close, I would sit alone on the end of the dock with my legs over the edge, letting the water swirl around them and soothe my tired feet.

I would gaze toward the mountains and watch the sun sink behind them. I would bathe in the mirage of color that reached out from the sky. The lake would turn pink, violet, copper, and gold. I would catch my breath as I beheld the natural painting that inspired so much feeling within me.

Then the image, as if it were afraid to give too much pleasure, would retreat to the mountains. Darkness would settle and a silent calm would come over the lake. Occasionally I would hear a canoe slipping through the shadows or the splash of a fish jumping. Then all would be still. I would quietly stand up and tip-toe up to the house, careful not to disturb the peacefulness.

When I entered the house, I would immediately be surrounded with laughter and chatter. My great aunt would always be sitting in her wicker chair concentrating on a crossword puzzle and would look up at me with a knowing look and smile.

After dinner my cousins, my brother, and I would pull on wool sweaters, gather up a flashlight and a container, and head for what was by day the golf course, by night—hunting grounds. Our voices would be reduced to whispers that were barely audible and our feet would hardly move one in front of the other. When we spied our victims, we would slowly move into the circle of light formed by flashlights and approach. When close enough we would lunge and pull out of its hole a long, fat nightcrawler. Hours were spent at this, and we caught one after another. They were to be bait for the next day. When we finally tired of this game, it would be late.

We would slowly return to the house, too tired to run. After cleaning up in the washtub and brushing my teeth with bottled spring water, I would drag myself up the creaky stairs. I would cast my tired eyes over the balcony and let them come to a rest on the deer head. It protruded from a hand-built chimney made of stone and below it hung guns that had been there for decades.

I would shuffle down the hall, undress, and slip in between the sweet smelling sheets. The broken-down cot felt so wonderful and allowed my muscles to release their final grasp. I allowed the weight of my eyelids to shut them. I listened for a moment to the voices floating over the wall that didn't quite reach the ceiling. Then I drifted off, knowing that I would be awakened early the next morning by birds chirping, by delicious smells from the kitchen, and with the sunshine warming my face.

Again, Jane did not write elaborate comments on the paper and made few editing marks; most of the job had already been done by talking in the conferences. The piece had been through a number of revisions before it reached this stage. Now on the final product, all Jane writes is: "A-. Images are wonderful!"

In our talks, Jane discussed at some length about the strength of the paper:

> It is unusual for our students not to have cliches, to find language uniquely their own, because that is embedded in their life. I like the line "the unkempt lakehouse with the shaggy lawn and ancient appliances." I like the line as simple as "late afternoons we usually spent climbing trees and exploring the woods where it was cool." The best writing is simple and clear, you don't have to use big words. I like her play with the color: "I would bathe in the mirage of color that reached out from the sky. The lake would turn pink, violet, copper and gold." That's very unusual. It's personification, but it's very natural. It is not contrived. This came out of her again and again revising her pieces, and finally for the first time [she] felt comfortable to let her writing happen without trying to formalize it, to make it into an essay.

The writing has its own natural voice, its own language, and its own natural form. That, in Jane's judgment, is good writing.

CHAPTER 2

Four Teachers and Six Pieces (Part 2)

The second round of discussion was among the four principal teachers on the six selected pieces, three from each country. They were invited first to comment on the six pieces, orally or in writing, assuming the pieces were written by their own students and doing what they would normally do. Then they were asked to respond to others' different evaluations brought to their attention by the researcher.

All the teachers, except for Jane, delivered grades. Chinese teachers used a percentage system (grades under 60 are failing grades), and American teachers used the letter system of A to F (grades under C are below the average). Grades, however, are not useful evaluative indices in comparative studies, not only because the grading systems are different between the two countries, but the value of grades varies drastically from one teacher to another even within the same country. Nevertheless, they are worth looking at. The fact that "There is an Old Lady" receives a perfect 100 from Mr. Zhang and a B from Jack shows clearly their different assessment of the same paper. Grades also have good referential values if we look at the grade fluctuation of one teacher assigned to the six pieces; teachers are usually fairly consistent in their own grading. That Mr. Wang assigns a grade of 82 to "Beat Them 'til They're Black and Blue" yet 83 to "Untitled II (Summer Camp)," whereas Jack gives the first piece an A and the second a hesitant B+, illustrates graphically what good writing means for each.

After presenting each teachers' comments on a piece, I would reflect briefly on their comments and then return to the teachers, meeting in person or through correspondence, with questions on issues where they differed. I posed the questions either to the teacher who selected the piece or to the teacher(s) who showed different perspectives on them. Although I tried to hold a separate discussion on each issue, the issues were so closely intertwined that often the discussion of one subject extended or shifted to another. As we discussed the question of contrivance, for example, the question of form and style became critical, and when I inquired into some teachers' views on effective endings, their perception on what is "true" or "phony" reemerged.

What it became was a dialogue among the four teachers, who never met one another. So this part, instead of moving from one country to the other, is organized around the pieces and the issues they raised. Setting up a topic for each segment is more out of the need for an accessible form than an accurate representation of reality, for it has the obvious problem of sidestepping the intricate connections among the issues. The world is intricate and chaotic, despite a researcher's effort to streamline it.

The four principal teachers' discussion of the six pieces provides a good sampling of the views on "good writing" in the two countries. Furthermore, they were ethnographers of their own cultures when they explored the social, political, and historical circumstances that have shaped the criteria for "good writing."

"BEAT THEM 'TIL THEY'RE BLACK AND BLUE" (REFERRED TO AS "GRANDPA" IN THE DISCUSSION)

Teachers' Comments

JACK: (Grade: A.) Comments in chapter 1.

JANE: "There are lines in this paper that go far beyond others' attempts to come up with a philosophy. It sees deeper. 'It was like he had willfully erased that part of his life,' is really a strong line. 'Some deeper awareness told me to be content with his stories, . . .' and it comes back to mother at the end, 'She was a stranger in the house she grew up in.' The writer goes beyond the scent of the pipe to prove her perception of her grandfather through her mother's life. Strong use of language. Yes. Is that rhyme original? 'If they do, take your shoe, and beat them 'til they're black and blue.' It must be added by her grandfather."

MR. WANG: (Grade: 82.) Final comments: "Your grandfather is really a bit strange, but he is still a lovable person. You aptly describe his temperament and personality. The scene in which your grandfather sat at your bedside, smoking a pipe and telling stories, is written with such affection that I felt I was there too. The fifth and sixth paragraphs are too simple; they should be further developed, because they tell about an important part of grandpa's character."

In the margins, he comments on the first paragraph ("The description of his physical appearance is very vivid") and on the fourth paragraph, where the narrator waited in bed for grandpa's footsteps ("the psychology is realistic").

In the discussion, he further elaborated his criticism: The fifth and sixth paragraphs describe grandfather's past, and before those, the writer has mentioned that he had mellowed with age. But how did his disposition change from being severe to loving? Little is said in the paper. That process of his change could be described in the fifth and sixth paragraphs, but the writer does not go into it. There seems to be some barrier between the grandfather and mother, but it is not explained, and we don't know what really happened. The writer only says that she "filled the empty spaces with make-believe stories," but that is not enough. So there is a gap; the story is not complete.

MR. ZHANG: (Grade: 75.) Final comments: "The depiction of his physical appearance, a simple account of his past, carefully selected details, and his contrastive attitudes towards his own daughter and granddaughter, all these portray an eccentric old farmer. His image is vivid and fascinating. But what is the significance of presenting such a character and his story? Writing is for educating and molding people's minds. It should, first and foremost, have meaning."

Mr. Zhang further stresses the last point in his letters: "I don't know what the young writer is trying to say to the reader, what exactly the theme of the paper is. Although the piece brims with feelings and expresses well her love for Grandpa, what kind of positive effect does the piece as a whole have on the reader? I don't see any.

"At first glance, it must appear ridiculous to use the strict Chinese moral standards laid down by our ancestors to measure the writing of those care-free American kids. Yet I believe 'writing is the vehicle of Tao' is a universal principle. Isn't it true that the three hundred and eight free verses that make up Whitman's *Leaves of Grass* sing the praises of the ordinary people and their optimism and strikes at the hypocrisy of bourgeois democracy? Isn't it true that Mark Twain attacks, though implicitly, slavery in *Huckleberry Finn?* And do not Hemingway's works, like *The Old Man and the Sea,* imbued with admiration for the working people, express his pursuit of man's high ideals?"

Li's Reflection

Both Jack and Jane applauded "Grandpa" as a piece of superior quality, yet this assessment was not shared by Mr. Wang and Mr. Zhang, who graded the paper 82 and 75 respectively. Their much lower estimation of the paper, it seems, resulted from their different reading of what the writer was trying to accomplish with the piece. Both Mr. Wang and Mr.

Zhang read "Grandpa" as a character profile of an eccentric farmer. Very impressed as they both were by the student's skill of vivid characterization, they found the piece fell short of what they thought a good character profile should accomplish. Mr. Wang was unsatisfied with what he saw as a "gap" in the story, for the author failed to explain the relationship between the grandfather and the mother. Mr. Zhang's dissatisfaction with the piece went deeper: he questioned the significance of presenting such a strange and unfathomable character. Jane's admiration for the piece's philosophical depth sounded a lonely voice among the three. I relayed the Chinese teachers' questions to Jack.

What is the Point?

LI: The Chinese teachers raised a number of questions about the piece: What is really happening between the grandfather and mother? What changed the old man from being severe to gentle? Why does the author mention the problematic relationship between grandpa and mother yet not go into it? What do you say to them?

JACK: Responding to the piece would be difficult for people who were not raised in contemporary America. Even older Americans, like the people of our grandparents' generation, will have a hard time with it, because it does not come to a clear resolution. In fact it is very ambiguous as to what factor in the man's life made him feel differently about the granddaughter than the daughter.

From the contemporary American point of view, Americans would see the situation as too complicated and too individualistic for us to make a judgment, and it would be just, "These things happen to people, and we can't figure them out," and he might not even know himself what factor has caused that. This is the understanding people have today of all the influences on our lives. In a way, that's the point of the paper. The point is that the dramatic difference between his reaction to his daughter and his granddaughter shows something mysterious about transformation of people's lives, and it is beyond our full grasp. Although Americans are as fond as any other people in the world about looking into psychology and we are so up to our eyeballs with psychology on our television talk shows, Oprah, Donahue, all trying to explain human behavior, a lot of more sophisticated Americans like to believe that we are being vain and arrogant to think we can decipher human motivation. So this paper really deals with that. When we get to the end, she said, "Unknown to me then," she stresses that these were unknowns, that "each night mother would come to kiss me good night. She and her father would pass each other in the hall, never touching, never loving." That passage helps us to understand that the author deliberately leaves us nebulous, amorphous, because she did not know. Just like two ships passing each other in the night, father and daughter passed each other in the night, and communication remains distant and cold. And she, the granddaughter who wrote this, does not recognize nor understand the problems either. So it is a recognition of the gulfs that separate people. It is simply a statement of the sadness of it. She does not say it is sad, only this is the way it happens in life. If she had said that, it would probably be more pleasing either to an older audience or to an audience outside the United States.

To sophisticated American readers we very often prefer that we readers draw that conclusion, and it has got to be well enough written so the readers will ask the right questions. If people, if Chinese teachers reading this, ask why this transformation took place, why the author does not direct us to the cause, they are asking all the right questions, but they are frustrated by the lack of answers. Many times we would feel the same.

LI: If, as you mentioned before, aesthetics is secondary in writing and meaning comes first, what is the value of a piece like this, which describes an old farmer who, as you said, may have physically abused his daughter?

JACK: This is the tradition in America for previous generations, and it is the tradition in many other cultures, that if a piece is worth writing, it is worth having a point. I agree with that. I think a piece should have a transcendent theme. We don't want just an amusing story, but a story that has implications for people at large. Then what is the point of this story? Well, the point is life is unexplainable and inexplicable in certain ways. I think in many ways Americans are inclined now to accept more of the moral gray areas, partly because America in the last twenty-five years has lost a sense of absolute values, and in many ways that is the tragedy of the United States. In order to be the open, flexible society in which we can live in peace with one another, we have to be open to all cultures and religions, we very often have to bury our absolutes.

The reason why America functions and survives, hasn't dissolved, is largely because there is tolerance of differences. But in order to tolerate differences, we have to accept that there aren't absolute universal truths. That's difficult for me as a Christian. I have to accept certain universal truths, what is right and what it wrong, but sometimes I have to accept that they are not culturally and socially acceptable by everybody else, and I have to live with that. This paper deals with that attitude.

LI (*talking with Jane*): Do you think the paper has a meaningful theme?

JANE: It is not my place to tell the student what to write, what not to. Once a student in my class wrote about drug abuse. It is my place to help him and ask, "What are you trying to say about this drug experience?"

LI: You are a teacher. What's wrong for you to tell the student, "You should not use drugs"?

JANE: The student has the right to. It is my place to let the students express themselves as effectively as they can, regardless of my opinion of the topic. We are not supposed to give values. I am much more directive asking students to think carefully about the values in literature, about how they would respond to those values. But with writing, we are not trying to produce a group of people who all write the same way and have the same values. When the student engaged me in the conference about drugs, I finally said, "Don't you think for a second that I condone your use of drugs." He was shocked, because I had been so noncommittal about it. But I think we should allow them choices, and allow them to think independently. We can't say that we want them to learn to think, when what we really want them to do is to think just like us. This, in a way, is our moral dilemma.

UNTITLED 1
("TO A FRIEND")

Teachers' Comments

JANE: (Grade: A-.) Comments in chapter 1.

JACK: (Grade: B+.) "Oh, boy, I was very pleased with this paper. It is agonizing to go through, of course. The structure is great. It starts off with this powerful opening that 'The world is still going to revolve, the calendar pages are still going to turn, and life will still go on as usual for most everybody. That's why it makes me so mad that you committed suicide.' Here we have the honesty of the written voice. The spoken voice wouldn't have been so nicely crafted and polished, but it still sounds like the kid. She uses the word 'mad,' and some people would object to that. If you craft it, you should use angry, which is the right word, but there is a direct addressee, 'make me mad at you.' So I say, yeah, I would probably have said 'mad' instead of 'angry.' It preserves some of the authenticity of the way this person would speak to his or her friend.

"It does very nicely on giving the background of their relationship. It does not give me incredibly personal glimpses, the quotes, or a particular day they went out together, but I don't think that is necessary. I get a picture of her friend, and the pain she feels for losing her. The only disappointment with this paper was when I got to the second page and saw it was pretty short. The final paragraph summarizes, 'I just want you to know that until we meet again, I love you, friend.' That's a good point to end on because the person feels better, the person has come to some resolution. That paragraph would work fine in a closing paragraph, if it were not so abrupt. There is no transition here. Because it labors a lot on the pain of this experience, yet it doesn't trace any of the process she went through to finally get to that point of ending with a little bit of forgiveness. But still it is nicely written except for that. I will still put it in B+, because I think many readers who read it would feel there is some part of this relationship underdeveloped."

MR. WANG: (Grade: 90.) Final written comments: "The entire piece emotes in the form of a direct conversation. It is written with tears and anguish. Your genuine love for your friend moves me deeply.

"With one after another rhetorical questions, you express to the fullest your grief for losing your best friend. There is no single word of flowery language or a false statement. This is natural beauty, genuine beauty! This is excellent! Would you like to be my friend?

"I wish you greater success with the next piece. I believe you will succeed, because you have a genuine heart."

Mr. Wang added a title to the piece before he sent its Chinese version to Mr. Zhang: "Listen to Me, My Friend. . . ." He fills in the margins of the paper with similar praises. For example, on the opening sentence, he comments, "Expresses your sincere feelings right from the beginning," on the second paragraph of recalling past friendship, "What affectionate memories!" and on the conclusion, "Brace up amid sorrow and pain, good!"

MR. ZHANG: (Grade: 85.) Written comments: "You write straight from the heart, expressing thoroughly your anguish, loss, remorse, confusion, and all the painful feelings. The 'anger' at your friend, which permeates the whole piece, for her act of suicide has the paradoxical effect of showing your intense love for her. Such an unusual way of expression shows powerfully the pain in your heart of hearts. But the piece could be more specific in content, especially the basis of your friendship needs to be explained more. Only then will the feelings expressed be more fully accepted by the reader."

Li's Reflection

It is interesting that all three teachers were deeply moved by the intense emotion of the piece. Yet Mr. Wang and Mr. Zhang liked the piece better than "Grandpa," both giving it a higher grade. (Mr. Wang graded it 90, compared with his grade of 82 for "Grandpa"; Mr. Zhang graded it 85 compared with his 75 for the previous piece.) Mr. Wang was most effusive in his praise, and Mr. Zhang and Jack were equally impressed, although they would like certain parts of the piece to be further developed. Ironically, that is not what this piece was supposed to accomplish. Jane warned, when first introducing the piece, that its purpose was, "not to emote, but to persuade," presumably to dissuade potential victims of suicide by showing them the pain their act could cause to their friends.

I am immediately struck by two questions: first, why did the Chinese teachers, Mr. Wang in particular, give such high grades to a piece explosive with emotions yet not as well written as "Grandpa" from a stylistic point of view? What is the value of writing that functions to emote personal feelings? Second, if the Chinese teachers like a piece that expresses agonizing feelings so much, why is it that few student papers they selected reach such emotional depth? I personally believe it has to do with the subject matter. "To a Friend" deals with a very private part of the author's life, yet "Me, Before and After the Exam," which is as private as I could get with all the Chinese pieces I have collected, deals with a subject matter that belongs to the public domain of the author's life: taking exams, which she already discussed with her friend and mother. Why are Chinese students' personal narratives so impersonal?

Qing is a term that keeps coming up in the Chinese teachers' talks. It does not have an exact equivalent in English; *qing* can mean feelings, sentiments, passion, love, or sexuality, and it can also refer to the emotional appeal of a piece of writing. But it does not have the negative connotation that "sentimentality" often carries in the English language, neither the manipulative overtone that "emotional appeal" often implies. It is the opposite of intellect, rationality, reason, and is close to the Western concept of heart, intuition, and other nonreasoning faculties of a healthy human being. The following discussion is about the issue of writing about emotion.

"Qing" and "Sentimentality"

LI (*to Mr. Wang*): You seem really moved by the piece "To a Friend" and gave it a higher grade than "Grandpa." What is the value of a piece just pouring out one's personal grief?

MR. WANG: This is in Chinese literary tradition from the very start. The first poem ever recorded in Chinese literature is a poem of *qing*:

> Sea-hawks are calling
> By the river board.
> . . .
>
> A modest sweet maid
> He seeks dark and light.
> Seeking her in vain
> Dark and light he yearns.

The main purpose of writing poetry in ancient times was to express one's emotions, to say in writing things you can't say in life. That was how literature in China started. Tang *shi* and Song *ci*[1] were not written for publication as people nowadays do. They were written for the poets themselves or their friends, expressing and sharing their private feelings, unless there were important political incidents, like the "An Shi Mutiny,"[2] that so much disrupted their lives that they wrote on public topics. It was not until Ming and Qing,[3] the last two dynasties, that novels began to gain popularity in China, and the nature of writing became more public.

Qing has great persuasive powers. *Li* (reason) is inseparable from *qing*: *qing* is couched in *li*, and *li* is couched in *qing*. They cannot be separated. *Li* (reason) is different from *lizhi* (rational). Being rational, one is emotionally controlled, somber, composed, exercising only intellectual and reasoning faculties. Reason, however, deals with truths. Truths, though existing in objectivity, are approached and understood only through subjectivity. Truths should be learned with passion and conviction. This is stressed as early as Confucius's time, when it was said that good writing should be excellent in both *qing* and arguments [*qing2 wen1 bing4 mao4*]. So according to the Chinese traditional point of view, you cannot produce powerful writing if you do not feel strongly about the truth. If the writer is not excited about the topic, how can he produce exciting works?

On the other hand, it has always been dangerous to write about one's true feelings in China in the realm of politics. When Emperor Li Shi-ming was in power, anyone who used the word *ming* could be executed, because that word was part of his name. In the Qing Dynasty, a poet was beheaded for writing, "Fresh[4] wind does not read characters. Why should you ruffle my book?" The only place where writers can be true to their feelings is when they write about nature, about their friends, and about art. I dare say Chinese love poems are the best in the world. The appeal of great poet Su Tong-po's[5] poem in memory of his deceased wife has remained undiminished after almost a millennium, because it expresses his genuine grief and undying affection for his wife. *Qing* is part of virtue; the expression of *qing* is, in the end, an expression of our admiration for lofty ideas and morality. Genuine emotions have the power to affect readers, and it is an important means for human understanding and connection because universal feelings resonate with all readers.

It may also have to do with the Chinese national temperament. Because our emotions have been so suppressed in public life for so long, we have become emotionally vulnerable inside and are prone to more emotional writing. What is written in this piece hits me so strongly that I was on the verge of tears when reading.

I graded it highly, because I believe that writing should come straight from the heart and that we should write with passion, and that is what this piece does.

MR. ZHANG (*responding to the same question*): Zhuangzi[6] says, "Without sincerity, there is no power to move. A forced cry, though sorrowful, does not sadden; pretended rage, though grim, does not inspire awe." Bai juyi, also points out, "To touch the heart, nothing compares to *qing*." We all respond to *qing* if it is sincere and comes from the heart; affected and exaggerated *qing*, like moaning and groaning without being sick, won't work. This piece shows genuine feelings, which makes it so powerful and moving.

LI (*to Jack*): You seem to be deeply moved by the piece "To a Friend," but do you think some people may think it too sentimental? Why does the term "sentimental" have such a derogatory connotation in this country?

JACK: Since the Vietnam War, people in this country have become cynical in many ways, and this aversion to sentiment is one of them. Sentimentalism is perceived as purposely creating or evoking in people a beautiful, emotional response to something they consider lovely and endearing. Many Americans today chuckle at that. They think it ridiculous, because it presents a phony impression of how things are.

LI: Do you mean that Americans suppress their emotional expression?

JACK: No. People are more likely to express emotions like rage, contempt, or truly vulnerable emotions, those like sorrow, loneliness, despair. Those are perceived as honest feelings. American democratic principles have so overly inflated the American individualist ego that we think everything is our right. Everything that bugs me, bothers me, is an infringement on my right, and it is my right to tell you exactly how I am thinking about it, which tends to be negative emotions.

Now there is a counter-movement, because people are feeling so battered by a society that is so negative, and so self-centered. Women have support groups, and men now are doing all this drum-beating to get back the feelings that bound us with one another. When there is a beautiful story, for example "Driving Miss Daisy," it captures the American imagination right away. The movie, as well as the novel, is very very powerful. It is honest, showing both the negative and the positive qualities, but clearly it evokes sentiments of nostalgia and care and love, and all that.

LI: I have not read many modern novels like that.

JACK: No, but in popular literature, Harlequin romance stories always sell well, along with murder mysteries and science fiction. But they have appealed more to the working class than to the upper-crust readers. They are a balance to that upper-crust literature. I read recently a romance called *Possession*.[7] It is a story about two writers, a man and a woman in the nineteenth century, who corresponded with each other by writing poetry back and forth. It is very difficult reading, with all kinds of allusions to poets of the nineteenth century, but it is a romance, very sentimental and touching.

LI: Is the book viewed as sentimental?

JACK: I don't think so, because it is so scholarly and esoteric, and that somehow gives it credence. So it has to be highly sophisticated to get away with that.

LI (*to Mr. Zhang*): Students are very good at taking cues from the teacher. If most Chinese teachers are, like you, coming from a tradition that highly regards the expression of *qing,* why is it that few Chinese students write about very private feelings, feelings that come from the deepest part of their hearts?

MR. ZHANG: That is a very good question. "Words express the intent of the heart," and students should open themselves up in writing, yet that rarely happens in today's China. I personally think this is the result of "exam education." Talking about taking cues, both students and teachers have to take cues from the college entrance exams. If we look at all the composition topics from the college entrance exams in the last ten years, disregarding what happened before the Cultural Revolution, the students were either asked to compose on an assigned topic or on provided prompts; topics have always been predetermined or narrowly defined. In the classroom, most teachers model their teaching on the entrance exam and ask the students to improvise on assigned topics. Where then is the place for students to "express the intent of the heart"? Many students fill their writing with "phony talk, big talk, and empty talk." The exam system is the cause of all this. In recent years, a uniform textbook has been used for Chinese classes throughout the nation, and after each unit of texts, the textbook provides exercises and topics for student composition. Rarely is there opportunity for students to choose their own topics. Composing on supplied prompts and topics certainly has its role in writing exercises and in exams, yet an inevitable result is that students are being trained to write only what they are asked to write, not what they want to write.

If you want to find writing that comes from the heart, the only place is student diaries and journals—there you will see a different world. In the early sixties I had a chance to look into that world. National politics, personal concerns, nothing was held back; joy, anger, sorrow, all emotions were let out. Words on paper came alive with flesh and blood; their writing was real and fascinating. If there was an ideological problem, the teacher wrote to the student or talked with them to exchange thoughts and give guidance or help. Teachers were equals, not ideological doorkeepers. We did not report what was revealed in the student writing. If that happened, the student would clam up immediately.

Some teachers and people with foresight have long noticed these problems and cried out for reform. Respected educator Ye Sheng-tao suggested, "We should understand the students and assign topics close to their hearts." Model teacher Hong Yu-li appealed, "Be bold and let the students write themselves." I think problems caused by "exam education" will be solved gradually, and we will have more and more student writing coming from heart.

There is another factor, though, concerning the choice of topics. Chinese tradition sets strict moral codes for young people's behavior. To speak ill of one's parents or siblings or to wash the family's dirty linen in public is considered improper and disgraceful. How can students write about very personal topics? Also, politically you are not supposed to write about the seamy side of the society, because that would "distort reality." What is left for the student to write about is very limited.

UNTITLED 2
("SUMMER CAMP")

Teachers' Comments

JANE: (Grade: A-.) Comments in chapter 1.

JACK: (Grade: B+ or B.) "This paper is such a considerable departure from the paper yesterday, 'To a Friend,' as we got into the discussion of honesty. This one is an attempt by the student to be literary, a movement far away from one's natural voice to want to sound like a writer. 'Then the image, as if it were afraid to give too much pleasure, would retreat to the mountains.' It sounds phony.

"Overall, I would say that's my only objection to it. But I will be very careful how I handle this, because it could be the end of the student's whole writing experience if I give a B on this paper and say that it is phony or dishonest language. That will be a terrible setback. I may be inclined to hike it a little bit and give it B+. I would say it is quite lovely for the capacity you have shown and it is crafted in certain ways, but let's look at some contemporary writers. Such style leads you away from what is good in your natural voice."

[LI: What's the point of the paper?] "It states in the opening, 'With the arrival of summer, my thoughts would turn towards the unkempt lake house . . . but it was a refuge from the modern, fast-paced world.' So from that standpoint, this person is trying to show that he needs that experience in his memory to be able to distance himself from the pressures and the pace of our society today and be more connected with nature. I can identify with that."

[LI: How about its structure?] "The structure is very good. I have no problem with that at all. It starts off with a general reference to how the author felt about that time, and then he goes into details. Each one is interesting to hear about: going off with the father and just spending the time alone, reflecting, looking at nature, and trips on the canoe and going to bed in this house which is like one of those old-fashioned log cabins. I thought it was vivid. I can picture them. Then it just goes through a day and ends with waking up in the morning with birds chirping. As a descriptive piece and a reflection of the past, it works nicely."

MR. WANG: (Grade: 84 -1, one point deducted for two typing errors —mine.) It tells about the activities in a day with completeness, and the order is clear, and it has all the four basic elements of a narrative we have been teaching in class: time, place, character, and incident. Certain passages are particularly well-written, even very poetic, for example, the passage about sitting at the dock at sunset: 'I would bathe in the mirage of color that reached out from the sky. The lake would turn pink, violet, copper and gold. I would catch my breath as I beheld the natural painting that inspired so much feeling within me.' The writer is admiring nature and indulging in a flight of fancy. This is what we call 'the blending of emotions and scenery' [qing2 jing3 jiao1 rong2]. [LI: What kind of emotion?] "The emotion is intoxication by the beauty of nature, the joy of being at one with nature. The language here is quite beautiful.

"There is one problem, though. We think narratives should have focus. Were there one or two incidents that were most memorable, even one piece of conversation, one activity that could be described in more detail? The piece as is is somewhat dull and flat for lack of any climax. For that, the piece cannot get a higher grade."

At the top of the paper, Mr. Wang writes, "How about titling the piece 'A Happy Day in Summer'?"

MR. ZHANG: (Grade: 65.) Written comments: "Perhaps because you spent two or three weeks every summer at the lakehouse as a child, and everything that happened there left a deep impression on you, some descriptions of the natural surrounding are written beautifully and movingly. It is indeed a good place to stay away from the fast pace of modern life.

"Yet looking at the structure of the piece as a whole, there lacks a thread that runs through from the beginning to the end. As a result, it is disorganized, and there is no connection between the opening and the ending. To some degree, it weakens the theme. When writing narrative, keep in mind that it should be structured as an integral whole."

Mr. Zhang also notices the absence of a title. He writes in the margin near the top: "A title is the 'eye' of a composition. A piece without a title affects the reader's comprehension." He suggests "Lakehouse in Summer." He also puts two circles beside the two passages that describe the scene at the dock and commends, "careful observation, keen experience, you have shown a vision." For the conclusion, he first comments on the last sentence, "[It] shows further the characteristics of idyllic life, and leaves an aftertaste in the mouth of the reader." And then he suggests, "Since the whole piece is about past memory, should it have an ending that echoes the opening?"

Mr. Zhang writes to me in later correspondence: "If this were written by a Chinese student, he or she probably would have cited the famous lines: 'The woods are quieter when cicadas din; the mountain is more peaceful with chirping birds' [*chan2 cao4 ling2 yu4 jing4, niao3 ming3 shan1 geng4 you1*]. The poem would add grace to the piece, but it would not have the same style as it does now, which is all written in the student's own language."

He also relates: "It is unfair to judge an American student's writing against our Chinese ideology, but in China the most common topic in students' writing today is to 'realize modernization,' which has become the aspiration of the whole nation and the guideline for our actions. Yet on the other side of the Pacific, an American kid wants to get away from 'the modern, fast-paced world.' How very strange this is!"

Li's Reflection

It is interesting to note that Jane chose this piece because it is "natural," "simple and clear," and does not use "big words." Yet Jack saw just the opposite: an example of moving away from the writer's "natural voice," of using outdated and phony language. It is also interesting that both Mr. Wang and Mr. Zhang picked up the same part from the piece for using "poetic" and "beautiful" language, the part to which both Jack and Jane paid little attention. It shows that although Jack and Jane do not make the same judgment about the use of language in a particular piece, they share the same criteria in theory. "Natural" language is to Jack and Jane what "beautiful" and "lyrical" language is to the Mr. Wang and Mr. Zhang.

Imitation is another issue. Jack criticized the piece for trying to "sound like a writer" by using highly literary words. I wonder what he would say to Mr. Zhang, who suggested a line of classic poem be added to the piece. The old saying, which is still very much alive in China, says that everyone can write, "If only one learns three-hundred poems from the Tang Dynasty by heart."

Another issue here is the question of form. Both Jack and Jane were pleased with the simple chronological structure of the piece, which is more natural for them, yet Mr. Wang and Mr. Zhang were dissatisfied. As their comments indicate, they believe good writing should focus on the one or two most significant events, linked together as a whole by a "thread," preferably a memorable image, and end with a conclusion that both wraps up the piece and reminds the reader of the opening. For the Chinese teachers, a glaring violation of the proper form with the American student writing was the absence of a title, an anomaly both of them noticed immediately, and both suggested a title to the writer. Yet neither Jack or Jane seem to have noticed.

The theme of the paper, too explicitly stated to be missed, is one that Jack could easily identify with, yet Mr. Zhang found hard to comprehend. Their attitudes, I surmise, are very typical of their own countrymen in this particular case, given the ideological climate in each country.

Since the larger issues of the form recurred in later discussions, here I confined the discussion to questions of the title and the criteria for good language.

What Has Happened to the Title?

LI (*to Jack*): Of all the American student compositions I have collected, more than twenty of them, only a few have titles, yet all the Chinese student writings have titles, not necessarily exciting ones, but a title is an integral part of every piece of their writing. What has happened to the title in American student writing?

JACK: This is my own theory. We have a lot of kids with all ranges of abilities resistant to titling things, because you have to draw from all of the details to get a single principal meaning as reflected in the title and to make the point. Yet there is so much resistance to telling somebody what it is about or what it means. Americans in the last twenty-five years are so much into the idea that everybody's opinion is as equal as everybody else's, so in writing we only repeat experience or present it as personal and avoid telling others what it is about. Then you wonder why talk, why write, why communicate. We certainly have gone to an extreme.

JANE (*responding to the same question*): This is interesting, because I do believe, as Murray showed me, that a title really can help define the purpose of the piece, and that's part of the process. Students have a hard time coming up with a title, so I used Don Murray's exercise and just say, "Well, let's just sit and write the first twenty-five phrases that come to mind." Inevitably they come up with one that they like. But I did not even realize that it was not there. Laziness. Listen [*laugh*] we are lucky to get anything from these students. These kids are just not trained to think about what they write. I think many of the students make leaps and bounds in attempting these pieces, not that I don't want them to do more with their writings.

Natural vs. Poetic

LI (*to Jack*): Did you think the writer of "Summer Camp" is dishonest? Why did you say he uses phony language?

JACK: No, I think it is this person's real feelings, but when it is translated into a language that is not part of this person's normal way of expression, it sounds phony.

I admired some of the descriptions, but when I got to lines like "I would cast my tired eyes over the balcony and let them come to a rest on the deer head." Oh, dear, "my tired eyes," it's old fashioned. It's nineteenth-century language, right out of the Victorian era to choose such a phrase. It seems to be too slavishly imitative of the phrasing that you associate with that period of the language.

LI: Why can't the student try to sound like a writer, or imitate others' language in their writing? Where else do they get their language if they don't imitate?

JACK: Freshness of expression is important in my judgment, especially in description. I find it very distressing if somebody talks about the long, lush, green grass, or even, in Kentucky words, blue grass. Somehow we anticipate green grass, and lush grass. Well, maybe you can use a better description, or use a metaphor for it, just avoid conventional ways of describing things.

"The broken-down cot felt so wonderful and allowed my muscles to release their final grasp." Nobody that I have met who was under seventy-five ever talked like that.

LI: But this is writing, not speech.

JACK: Ok, it is writing. If you send this to a publisher, you wouldn't get it published. "I allow the weight of my eyelids to shut then. I listened for a moment to the voices floating over the wall that didn't quite reach the ceiling." That is a situation in which the author has stopped to try to visualize it in a metaphorical manner, imagery of poetry and all that sort of thing.

LI: What is wrong trying to be poetic?

JACK: Poetry is a highly contrived art, and in a way we admire that, but it is no longer the literary medium by which the typical person communicates. I would say this piece falls in the direction of too much craft.

I said it is crafted, because of the value we currently place on a natural and honest voice. That's a value judgment of our society, especially in terms of what sells in public, what we read in the papers, the way we communicate. It is a funny thing, though. If it is judged by a group of high school students, they will give it an A. They will say that is impressive, because they are often impressed by beautiful wording.

We have this balance between striving to make a piece of art, a thing of beauty, idealized, better than the way we say it at the moment and the other side, just write the way we talk. It is on a continuum from one to ten, from gut-level honesty, like four letter words, whatever the way you say it, all the way to ten, which is you scrub it clean of everything to make it lofty. I tend to be happier when the balance falls between four and five. It is not necessary for a writer to write in his conversational voice, but a voice that readers would say that sounds like the way *this* writer would tell the story. So it is not so far removed from a person's natural language, but it is polished, perfected.

Should our voice be the same all the time? What I say about George Bush will be quite different if I talk to the Christian Women's Club annual convention from if I talk to a friend while I was fixing a car. Not the content; what I feel about George Bush will be consistent in both occasions. It will be a matter of how I phrase myself in a different situation, facing different audiences, playing a different role. I have multiple voices, and I think any writer does.

LI (*asking Mr. Wang*): Why do the Chinese teachers like the poetic language so much?

MR. WANG: There are historical and linguistic reasons. For centuries, whoever ruled China, free-thinking was taboo, and politics a risky topic, so Chinese men of letters were forced to channel their energy to the perfection of their techniques, and their writing mostly communed with nature, which for them epitomized beauty. In the past, poets vied with each other to produce the perfect verse, deliberating on every character and every line to conform to the tonal patterns and rhyme schemes to a tee. That tradition is still alive. Teachers still prefer writing that demonstrates a good grasp of vocabulary, history, and classic works, uses vivid imagery, and employs a variety of rhetorical devices. The use of the colloquial and the vulgar is considered a lack of elegance and beauty and is looked down upon.

There is also a linguistic reason. Chinese characters were pictographic at the beginning. For example, the character of water has flowing lines, the one for mountain resembles a rolling mountain range, and the character for tree literally grows roots. So even now people like writing that is beautiful visually. Symmetry is more beautiful than asymmetry; proverbs, which usually consist of four characters, are more pleasing to the eye than phrases of two or three characters. So a student who uses more proverbs tends to get higher grades.

Ye Shen-tao, who passed away only recently, is one of the most respected educators in China. He had long criticized teachers who encourage students to produce what he called "beauty texts," texts that appear and sound beautiful without substance, yet this practice is still common. Personally I encourage my students to feel more comfortable bringing the colloquial language into their writing and prefer a plain style, but I also appreciate more lyrical images and language.

MR. ZHANG (*responding to the same question*): Good writing, no matter what one writes about, should have "literary grace" [*wen2 cai3*; literally means "literary colors"]. Good language is drawn inevitably from two sources: either from our ancestors' works or from today's everyday fresh oral language. The former is acquired by reading extensively good classic works. Student writing is impoverished if students fail to draw on both sources.

LI: Are you concerned that students may slavishly imitate what they memorized from classic works and lose their natural voices? Is it boring if everybody talks the same?

MR. ZHANG: This issue should be looked at dialectically. First of all, language is a means of communication. If a word or phrase is not imitated and used by a lot of people, how can language be the medium of the community? Secondly, we have different criteria for professional writers and students. A professional writer who imitates others' style and repeats the same word too often is not a good writer. But students are like apprentices, still learning the craft, and imitation is one way to learn. Students cannot invent words or expressions; they learn those things from reading or from the environment they live in. Of course, high-school students often mindlessly imitate terms they consider "hot." In the last few years, students have suddenly become very fond of the phrase "the sense of loss," and throw it in their writing a lot. That's why in our teaching we also stress that good writing should accurately reflect reality. We tell them to write about their real feelings about life and express them in their own words, and not to try to sound like everyone else, particularly not to try to sound like an adult. We are against using pompous language just to impress the reader. So, for us the question here is not imitation, but appropriateness. As long as they can use what they have learned appropriately, it is their language. You are worried that by using the same language we will all talk the same, or as Tsao Hsueh-chin, author of *Dream of the Red Chamber,* says that writing should avoid "a thousand people who all wear the same mask" *[qian1 ren2 yi1 mian4]*. Chinese language has such a rich pool of synonyms and antonyms, that scenario is very unlikely to happen. Actually the more vocabulary a student masters, the richer the feelings and ideas he will be able to express, the less likely they will all write the same.

LI: What if they all write green, lush grass if that is what they see?

MR. ZHANG: I don't see anything wrong with that if the grass is green and lush. As I said, the key is accuracy and appropriateness, not novelty.

LI (*asking Jane*): Some teachers feel this piece sounds phony, because it is too crafted. What is your response to that criticism?

JANE: Writing has to be a craft. I encourage students to play with language, but some kids are ready to do that, some are not. I encourage them to experiment with language, to try something that they don't think they can do. I am not trying to get them to break the rules of English; I am trying to get them to break their own barriers that language put on them. These kids, not primarily, but only speak in cliches. They don't think much. Everyday, everything is the same. Maybe it is our fault they are not in formal situations where they need to be articulate. I think I try to get them to do that. I say, "Your writing is just like your oral language," but I don't really mean that. What I really mean is that I want it to be as spontaneous as if they just get down ideas without thinking how to say it nicely, and then I want them to begin to craft it. Crafting starts with them beginning to look critically at what they have written. This piece is a nice attempt at craft.

"THERE WAS AN OLD LADY"
("OLD LADY")

Teachers' Comments

MR. WANG: (Grade: 86.) Comments in chapter 1.

MR. ZHANG: (Grade: 100.) Written comments: "The composition portrays a veteran who dedicated her whole life to the revolution, and delivers a distinct and profound theme. The writer delineates the character by showing her physical appearance and demeanor. The description of the surroundings also sets off the lady's character well. The process of coming to know the old lady is used as a thread to link the whole piece together, which follows a chronological order but is interrupted once in a while by some background information. It integrates narration, description, reflection, and the expression of emotions."

He further explains some of his comments in a letter: "The message sent by the piece, which portrays a character who sacrificed everything, including her own child, for the cause of revolution and then lived an ordinary life, has a profound meaning today when many people, including some party veterans, are abusing their power for personal gains.

"The straight back of the old lady, still straight after the talk about her lost son had obviously shaken her, leaves an indelible impression on the mind of the reader. 'The towering French parasol trees' resemble her 'thin' and 'straight back' and her undaunted spirit. The cool shade of the trees in summer reminds me of the proverb 'One generation plants the trees under whose shade another generation rests.' All these descriptions help portray a strong and noble character.

"The introduction of a fat man at the end who always brags about his Revolutionary past sets such an effective contrast with the old lady that the reader comes to respect her even more, which further strengthens the theme. The final conclusion is like adding the eye to the dragon *[hua4 long2 dian3 jing1]*.

"The narrator's reaction, 'My mother always holds my hand tightly whenever we go downtown. You did not hold his hand, did you?' and her reflection, 'A hero in a child's mind is like . . ., well, the sculptures in front of the Monument to the Revolutionary Martyrs. How could she be one of them?' is written in a plain and natural language, like a child's speech.

"All considered, this piece is better written than anything ever produced by my own students, so I graded it 100."

JACK: (Grade: B.) Written comments: "What about the author's understanding of what constitutes a hero and the impact of this old woman on that perception?"

Jack likes parts of the piece: the description of the lady's appearance at the first meeting ("Nice.") and the conversation between the child and the lady ("Very touching, nicely narrated"). But he raises more questions. In the opening, he is confused as to what the "image" refers to: "Is she the image or the house? Misleading lead." He underlines "Now I know it was her disposition, but I did not know what to call it then" and suggests, "weak, omit?" With the part in which the narrator reflects hearing about the old lady's past, he remarks, "Focuses reader on a general concept: what does a hero 'look' like?" He is unsatisfied that the reflection does not go any further.

JANE (*Commenting while reading*): "Good description. 'Especially in summer, walking in the shade of French parasol trees. . . . Often some tiny violet flowers overgrew the wall and spread into the open space in front of our house.' But the 'later' syntax—later this, later that—does not sound good. I like the laughter—I think, why did they laugh? I like the statement of the individual, 'My mother always holds my hand tightly whenever we go downtown,' although the 'fat man with a big belly moved in, always bragging about . . .' Is that real? Is this a fiction or nonfiction?"

[LI: The assignment was to write about a good person that you know. It is supposed to be about one's real experience. Just assuming it is nonfiction, what would you say to the student?] "I would read the last paragraph aloud and ask her how it sounds. Would she keep the four 'later's'? Is it a choice that she likes? Was there a fat man? Or is it a contrivance to show something about her? [LI: What if I say, ok, I made this fat man up, because I feel it makes the piece better?] I would say, you don't need the fat man to show your point. The fact that the lady is no different from your grandmother makes the same point in a very subtle way. I think what is happening is sometimes they are trying to write so hard they lose sight of what is moving and what is not, and what motivates the piece in the first place.

"'She gives me strength and inspiration; she teaches me to be sincere' is not understated. I am not sure that tag is necessary. I am not even sure it is believable. Where is the woman being sincere? I believe her that the woman is affectionate and kind and an ordinary person or lets herself appear to be an ordinary person when she is actually an extraordinary person. But 'she teaches me to be sincere'—I don't think it is honest that something in the piece taught her that.

"I guess I see it as a strong piece. I like the descriptions of the lady and of the place. I like the door, yet the last line has got to go. That's not what comes through. It's like the moral of the story that the kid wants to add at the end. I can see the discovery that an ordinary old lady was a national hero would have a profound impact on a child, but that's what I want to see developed, as opposed to just saying it had a profound effect upon me. The reader does not need that. I think that's all that ending does.

"I am not sure the opening is as strong as it could be. It's well-written, but I think everybody can start with that line because that's where we begin, "Oh, gee, there is a memory in my mind and it is strong, so I will write about it." I think it takes much more creativity and decision-making to begin to play with leads after the piece is written. The image is at the beginning and the end, so it is a kind of formalized standard framework. It is an introduction, not a good lead."

[LI: How about the portrayal of the lady?] "It is not strong in my mind. I think there is a good attempt at it. I like 'straight back,' 'silver hair,' but 'faces cut with deep wrinkles, between the layers of which seeped profound kindness,' that is contrived. That is just the first sight of her. It is too soon, it is too contrived."

[LI: So what is your final suggestion for revision?] "I want to talk to her. I hope in the conversation, she will begin to talk about this woman, if she really feels strongly about her, and her image is really clear to her, because the image of that woman is not that sharp and clear in my mind. I will listen carefully to what she has to say about the woman, and I will say, 'You just gave me a clearer image that you did not give me in this piece. Could you get some of that down? Is there some more?' She went into the woman's home and had conversation with her, but I don't see the woman's home; I don't see anything in fact—I just see the door. I would say to the student, 'Do you want me to see inside the home, or is the door the most important image?' I will tell the student the things that strike me as vivid. I will try to give them my reader's response, so that they can decide.

"I really like this part, 'A hero in a child's mind is like . . .how could she be one of them?' Here seems to be the realization, but there is little internal reflection. I guess I would ask the student to go back to take that question and do some thinking about that on paper and see if it helps, and not try to write the piece or to try to make the piece work, but just to see what questions come out of that, 'What did she expect of a hero? What is a hero?' because the piece says that she learned something about human nature, about what a hero really is, and then go back to the writing and see if there is enough there."

Li's Reflection

I am surprised by the mismatched responses to this piece and how clearly the line of difference fell along the nationality of the teachers; although there are parts in the piece that all teachers liked—the conversation between the child and the old lady, and the reflection of what a hero is like—the overall evaluation of the piece could not differ more. Jack gave it a B, the lowest grade he has ever delivered, whereas Mr. Zhang gave it the highest and perfect grade of 100, for its outstanding portrayal of a veteran revolutionary and the delivery of a profound message, besides its other merits. Yet profundity is exactly what Jane and Jack considered the piece lacking. They both wanted the writer to reflect more on the critical question of what a hero is really like. Again that mismatch arose partly from the teachers' disagreement as to what the piece is trying to accomplish or what they think the piece should try to accomplish: Mr. Wang and Mr. Zhang's comments indicated that they saw the goal of this piece was to portray a noble woman, and for that, the writer did an outstanding job. Jack and Jane wanted the writer to turn inward, to focus on *her* understanding of the meaning of a hero, and found the piece stopped short of that goal.

The strongest criticism came from Jane, who considered the piece too contrived. Her criticism was based mainly on three of her observations: a formulaic structure, a moral tag that was mismatched with the body, and the intentional dramatization, particularly with the fat man at the end.

There are quite a number of issues involved here. The following section concentrates on the discussion of issues of characterization, contrivance, and form. The last two are closely related, because, as Jane points out, a too-formalized structure smells of contrivance. I leave the questions of subtlety and leads, which come up again later, to the next section. But first, Mr. Zhang talked about the Chinese way of characterization, which was triggered by my question on reflection.

The Internal and the External

LI (*to Mr. Zhang*): You have given "Old Lady" the unusual grade of 100, but the American teachers gave it a lower grade, because they think the author should be more reflective of what the experience means to her understanding of the hero. What do you say to those teachers?

MR. ZHANG: They probably want the narrator to dwell on her mental activities, maybe "the stream of consciousness," but that is not what we do. I have read Tolstoy's *Resurrection*. What I remember most clearly about that novel is the male protagonist's repentance after he heard the death of Maslova. Tolstoy spends an entire chapter, translated into five to six pages in Chinese, to describe his internal pain and remorse, which cleansed his soul and all that stuff. I asked several people what they thought of the chapter, and their answers showed that most Chinese readers find that chapter hard to go through and terribly boring, even though they knew that it is a world classic. It is all internal monologue, no conversation, no movement, no description of the natural surroundings. That is not the way we Chinese write about a character's internal world.

We use speech or external action to express what is going on inside the character. In *Waterside*,[8] for example, what the character thinks is directly stated, like "Wu Song thinks so on and so forth," with only a few simple sentences. Or their motive is openly expressed in their speech or through describing the character's actions. Let me show you another example in the textbook. Sun Li, one of the few founders of Chinese modern literature who is still alive and in good health, is the author of the lyrical prose "Lotus-flower Lake" *[He2 Hua1 Dian4]*. It has been included in every Chinese textbook for decades as a fine model of prose. When he describes the mind of Shuisheng's wife, he does not use a long internal monologue like Tolstoy. He writes, "When Shuisheng's wife heard that after the meeting, Shuisheng was going to leave home to join the army to receive training in order to fight the Japanese, for a second, the woman's fingers quivered." Shuisheng's wife was then knitting mats with reed stalks, so the writer continues, "Maybe the end of the reed stalk had hurt her fingers." This scene is regarded as one of the best descriptions of the character's mind in the history of modern Chinese literature. Every time I taught this short prose, the students were greatly excited and inspired by this scene. This is absolutely a Chinese style. Sun Li does not spend pages to write how much pain Shuisheng's wife felt, how she was unwilling to let her husband go; all he mentions is "for a second, the woman's fingers quivered," and let the reader imagine how she really felt. The author of "Old Lady" says she went back to visit the lane and noticed the towering trees. There is enough for the reader to imagine what an impact the old lady had on her, and she does not need to dwell on it or start an internal monologue. Such narrative is reserved, which is in keeping with Chinese temperament. Chinese readers like such descriptions, and when they read the internal monologues like in *Resur-*

rection, they tend to skip them to find out the next development of the story. Maybe this has to do with aesthetic taste or the reader's level of education, but I think it has more to do with our tradition.

Traditional Form, a Liability?

LI (*to Jane*): You want the students to discover forms for themselves. But they are students, they are learning like apprentices. Why can't the teacher just teach them the forms?

JANE: I guess the traditional training I had did not teach me to think like a writer. Teaching writing is to teach them to be conscious of the choices they have, and I was not aware of my choices. Many of my students follow formats and really say nothing or don't know how to make choices about developing and what details to put in or take out. I think they become better writers for being able to. This is an excellent draft, I would like to get hold of the student. And that is the problem, making all these decisions about what the writer might do and might not do without the writer, I do not feel comfortable.

I show forms to my students, but we are not discussing as much about form as about "focus." I tell them, you have to make a decision as to what to say in this piece and then you have to follow it through.

I don't believe in teaching form first, because it is not going to do anything but destroy everything I try to get them to learn. Because these kids can follow exactly what the teacher asks them to do, but they have to learn that writing comes from themselves, whether it's about a book, about an issue, or about personal experience. When they leave school, I don't like that they can write five-paragraph essays, but that they believe they can write. I know they will be ready to be shot down in other writing courses, but I believe they are ready to take criticism.

I don't say this to others because I feel I could be caught short by people who want to teach forms. They will say, "What? You don't teach form?" Then I think, all right, so I am not teaching what I am supposed to be teaching, but, from seeing their writing before, I know that they are learning.

Form is important, but form that is organic could be as strong as form that is taught. If the organization does not exist, I'll take a scissors and cut out all the paragraphs and say to the student, "Take these, go home and play with them." And then they begin making decisions. I have to encourage them and let them alone, encourage them and let them alone. Just let go.

It is a lot of work both on my part and theirs to trust spontaneous, nonjudgmental writing. All we do is free writing and let surprises happen, and learn to trust that they will happen.

LI (*to Mr. Zhang*): You find the structure of "Summer House" incomplete, because there is no connection between the opening and the ending, and you like the structure of "Old Lady," in which the same word, "image," is repeated in both the beginning and final paragraphs. Why is it important to have an ending that sort of correlates with the opening?

MR. ZHANG: We are different from the Americans. American kids' writing seems to drift a lot, just putting down what comes to their minds. There is no structure. Chinese traditionally attends to the art of composition. Confucius says, "Speech without style does not travel far," and *"wen2 zhi4 bing1 bing."* The latter is now used to describe someone who is properly dressed and has impeccable manners, but originally it meant writing should conform to the standard both in content and form.

For example, the first story in *Annals by Zuo (zuo3 zhuan4)*[9] is a short biography of a general called Zhen. The story begins with "At the outset, General Zhen married Wu Jiang in Sheng" and ends with "Thereafter, the mother and son got along as at the outset." The story is regarded as a model of composition not because of the story itself, but for its well-conceived structure, which begins and ends with exactly the same word, *"Chu"* (meaning, at the outset).

LI: But wouldn't it be better if the student can think of his own structure? How about cutting out the last paragraph, since it is not saying anything new?

MR. ZHANG: There is no one fixed form, but there are some basic forms. Basically we think a piece of writing should have four components: introduction, development, transition, and closure *[qi3 cheng2 zhuan3 he2].* I think this basic format is still valid because they are in accord with the way we think and are effective in expressing what we want to express.

I am talking about traditional structure, yet the student does not have to use it if it does not fit the content of the paper. Generally we believe that restating what is said at the beginning or related to the beginning at the end helps focus the paper. The piece is incomplete without the final paragraph, which sums up what the writer has learned from this. We have three thousand years of writing history and our ancestors have written so many books and generalized excellent approaches to writing. They are our valuable inheritance. Teachers have the responsibility to teach a student the successful writing experiences of our forefathers.

It is not that we refuse to accept new forms. Lu Xun employs "stream of consciousness" in his works, as does the contemporary writer Wang Meng. To be honest, I personally find works that use "stream of consciousness" hard to follow, and I am more comfortable with traditional and realistic works. Maybe because I was exposed to the traditional type first, and as we say, "First impressions last."

MR. WANG (*responding to the same question*): It is very unlikely that one would start a piece from a form; we all start from ideas or from some experience in life. We teach form mainly through reading. We believe the more one reads, the more models and forms one absorbs, the better you write. When you have assimilated all kinds of forms, you can easily find a form appropriate for your writing. Teachers give them recipes and students can select from and modify them, but they cannot cook well with no recipes at all.

It's like teaching a baby to walk; you first have to hold his hands, and then let him walk on his own. We teach students some approaches, like analogy, contrast, and ways of structuring writings, but these are not restrictions, only approaches or ways of writing. How a student actually writes is determined by his life experience, knowledge, his ability to think, and other factors.

Creativity is built on inheritance, on the valuable experience of the previous generations. Especially in a country like China that has a literary history of thousands of years, it is arrogant to think that one can surpass his predecessors without first learning from them. Besides, every era produces only one or two great writers, and China has not seen one in the last forty years.

Do Americans imitate others? They probably deny that in words, but they also have great writers. Their students also read those writers and are inevitably influenced by their works. They probably just do not recognize their influence.

What Is Honest?

LI (*asking Jane*): How do you judge whether a piece is contrived or not?

JANE: I think real honesty comes through. It is sincere; it is not contrived. But very often the student has to dig to find the real honesty behind the piece. It has to be their piece, not somebody else's. Writing has to start from self.

LI: Do you think that, at the same time, writing is a public act, and writers can't be just themselves?

JANE: But they have to explore more what they really think and what they really feel. I just spent five weeks getting them writing fast and furiously, so that they can't rework to make it sound good. They have to discover whether they have feelings at all, what they are, and what they think first. I do not make corrections, for once the process of correcting and editing and polishing begins, the writing stops. I act as mediator between the students and their subjects, in a nonjudgmental, encouraging, questioning way, to help them search more deeply about their own thinking. After they have discovered what they really have to say, then they can be directed to choose what audience they want to address and revise their writing accordingly. But again, revision is a matter of learning to make choices, not following a format handed down from the teacher. I ask questions as a reader would, rather than giving answers. This way they can develop a sense of audience and learn to ask the same questions. To produce honest writing, we have to let them take charge of their writing. It's not easy. It takes patience and trust on both our parts. I just assume students can explore more about their subject, focus, audience, purpose, meaning, language, organization, and they do. Once they have learned to make their own choices and decisions and stop relying on our answers, they become more independent thinkers and good writers.

LI (*to Jack*): What is honesty? Do you think the fat man at the end is contrived?

JACK: No, that does not bother me at all. All arts are contrived; poetry is highly contrived. It is very important for writers to deal with life, to be reflective, to look into themselves and the meaning of their lives. That's the whole purpose of writing as far as I am concerned. But that's not the whole thing; the other side of the coin is to communicate to other people about that. But certainly fifty percent of it is to come to grips with yourself. Writing is, above and beyond everything else, a means of communication. It is so American to say, oh, it does not matter, well-phrased or not, punctuation marks out of place or it's spelled wrong, the main thing is to somehow feel better, to learn something about yourself. That is damaging to a child, because it leaves them trapped inside themselves, all obsessed with how they feel, how they think without feeling they have a responsibility to deal with the outside world, to communicate with the outside world, to find truth with other people.

We have such an obsession in our culture now with honesty, an honesty I see defined as things are much more inferior than they are presented. One of the worst words we use nowadays is image, people's image. Everyone is very critical and cynical about image. So honesty is turned into a cynical concept. I would have to say the pendulum has swung much too far in the direction of honesty, and not enough in terms of civility. We need to bring back the balance, and the balance is very much reflected in the way people evaluate writing in these days.

LI: But you also think it very important to have an honest voice.

JACK: Oh, sure. It's not either-or, it's balance.

LI (*to Mr. Wang*): Do you think good writing should be honest? Do you think "Old Lady" is an honest piece?

MR. WANG: Should writing be honest? No doubt about it. As I said, we don't just teach writing for writing's sake; instead, through writing, we teach the student how to be a useful person to the society. Of the three criteria for good writing—real, good, and beautiful—real comes first. Without the real, the good and the beautiful are ill-founded. To be real is to tell the truth, which is not only the prerequisite for a good piece of writing, but for being a man. If I find falsehood in my students' writing, I would point it out, of course, in a way that would not hurt the student's feelings. Our education would be a big failure if we didn't set down that principle. But in this case there is no reason to suspect that the student is being dishonest.

LI (*to Mr. Zhang*): You said you like realistic works, but what do you mean by realistic? Do you think it is important for the students to be honest in their writing?

MR. ZHANG: Realistic works are works that are true to reality. Du Fu, for example, is a realistic poet, because he was more objective in his time. In his poems he quite truthfully records the war-ridden life of the people around the time of the "An Shi Mutinies," so now we can learn about the society during that time through his poems. That's why his poems are often referred to as "poems of history." If he wrote eulogies that presented a false picture of peace and prosperity, then he would not be such a great realistic writer.

Generally, we expect the student to write about real people, real incidents, and real feelings in their personal narratives. But the criterion is somehow different for creative writing, which draws from real life but is more artistic than real life. According to Marxist Realism, a writer who can distill from life, whose work is more typical of mundane reality, is closest to truth. As long as the artistic creation is not far removed from what could actually happen in real life and does not violate common-sense logic, it is in line with Marxist Realism. From the teaching point of view, we want the students to write about their real experience, especially in their personal narratives, yet since students are just writing as a kind of exercise, we allow them to embellish their writing a little, under the condition that the stories are still believable. Actually in a composition exam, provided the writing is good, who would check out whether it is true or not?

"ME, BEFORE AND AFTER THE EXAM"
("EXAM")

Teachers' Comments

MR. WANG: Comments in chapter 1.

MR. ZHANG: (Grade: 95.) Written comments: "This is lyrical prose *[san3 wen2]* that expresses the writer's feelings elicited by an event in her life. The theme 'conquering self' is extraordinary, and the structure is also well conceived. The change of the narrator's feelings before and after the exam threads the piece together. It employs various means of expression, mingling narration, description with the expression of emotions. With a few touches, it also presents the characters around her with vividness. The language is simple and beautiful."

Mr. Zhang later further explains some of his comments in a letter: "The theme *[li4yi4]* of the piece is both new and superior to most student papers. It is new, because the narrator would rather pass up an exam, from which she may earn extra credit, to go to an ornithology test to be part of the effort to protect the environment. It shows that the present generation of high school students reject being crammed with exams and want to become well-developed people. The message that one should conquer oneself is one that is inspiring and uplifting. That's why I say it is 'superior.'

"The writer, by fusing the process of 'conquering self' with the scenes of sunset along a boulevard, creates a piece that has the beauty of poetry and painting.

"The piece is organized along the emotional changes the narrator underwent: first her confusion before the exam, then her mother's words and the scene of the sunset evoking in her feelings for nature, and finally the joy and relief after the exam. One climax following another, it presents its ideas in a clear and logical manner."

JACK: (Grade: A-.) Written comments: "The catharsis you went through is nicely presented. You made your own choice—a hard one—but with great sensitivity for the teacher of composition whom you respect. It implies your point well: you must take responsibility for your choice, but that involves cherished relationships, and such choices, when maturely made, aren't simple.

"You establish the conflict between the characters well. Your ambivalent attitude is effectively shown in your self-reflection as you walk the boulevard.

"The title is not subtle or metaphorical—could you consider another?"

In our discussion he elaborates on his comments: "This is an important catharsis for the person, and the person is at peace with the decision she made. She felt so sure of her decision finally that despite all the struggles along the way, she just knew that her teacher, whom she respects, will understand. To me that is what decision-making surely is all about. So I get the point. She implies this very well by showing the process she went through, just using the particular cases involved, not making a direct, general statement, so it has very strong power of subtle implications and that's why I marked it very high.

"The only reason why I will take off a little and not give her A is that there are a few moments that do not seem quite as strong. The very opening, 'The bell rang for class,' is just not a good beginning. I think the opening can be much stronger if it starts with the sentence in the third paragraph, 'I walked back and forth along the boulevard, recalling what happened in the class that morning.'

"The dialog is believable, for example, the cut-off dialogue. The paragraph I particularly admire is the one with the mother. I found it a very strong paragraph, because it brings in another factor of mature decision-making, that is, the influence of authority figures. If you are doing an essay on this subject of mature decision, you do consider the wisdom of people before you, the experience of other people, and you also consider the feelings of people involved and how much damage could be done, and write very explicitly about it. But instead she makes it very personal, and brings in all these things very subtly in those five paragraphs. The ambivalence comes back again and again, looking at the clouds disappearing.

"She uses a lot of atmospherics. She chooses to begin two paragraphs with atmospherics rather than directly come back to her mind. [Li: Do you like that?] I can buy that. Maybe I should add 'The atmospheric and setting also advance the theme through mood,' because that is definitely true.

"The last paragraph, 'The person I became was not the same person I was before the tests: free from hesitation, free from conflicts—my heart sings with joy! . . .' I would say that is not a paragraph that stands out to me as wonderful. Is all ambivalence erased? I think that held down a little bit my estimation, because it made it too neat at the end. I am not sure it is real either. I think it may be a feeling that is more pleasing to the reader to know that it is solved; you came out and you made a good decision and it was the right decision.

"The title of the story is not strong, because the tone of the paper is very much into symbolism: the birds, the ducks, the sunrise, the atmosphere, and then to come out to say, 'Me, before and after the exam' is very bland. It sounds like something in the seventh grade, very explicit, but the paper is very subtle and powerful. That puts you off."

JANE: "A lovely piece. The beginning is more standard, talking about Miss Lee. I love the image of sunset, 'like a dazzling beauty ready to depart, and whose beauty people were allowed to admire up to the last moment.' Lovely conversation about the mother and the saint, and the way she made decisions. She did not say how she made the decision about the test. She returned to the same scene again. It is wonderful here, the imagery of the ducks at the end."

[Li: Why do you like the scene of conversation with mother?] "It is very brief. The stroke of the loving hand, the words of the Indian saint, I read that twice to capture his wisdom, so I saw a loving, wise woman. We don't really see the teacher; the only thing I remember about the teacher is the bottles at the lunch, and the classmate was just busy and said something she obviously shouldn't consider too seriously. The mother is the deciding factor; she gave her the answer: to conquer herself, and that was the struggle.

"She does well integrating those three scenes with people and very briefly, and still make that sunset, which can be very conventional, work very well towards the end. She did the ending in a lovely way. The beginning is pretty conventional, 'The bell for class rang.' I like the way she uses one line. My students wouldn't think to do that. It's fine, but it's not moving like the other parts. I might ask her to play around with other ways to open this. I might ask her to find a line that she really liked, and ask her what she will do if she begins with that line and how the piece would be different."

[LI: How about the atmospherics? Do you encourage your students to do that?] "No. Most of them like to write that stuff, and very often it doesn't work, very cliche. But it is not cliche here. She gives the sunset new meaning. It helps her to make the decision. The ducks, though, surprised me. Birds have a different meaning, but happy ducks? I guess maybe that's what Donald Duck did to us. I assume it was part of her culture's difference from my students'.

"I find it a very important theme for me and for my students. It is about the process of making decisions. Sometimes they are struggling and they are unaware of the real dilemma they are in. I really think it is a very important theme that I encourage them to write about when they come upon this sort of thing.

"It is kind of unstructured. I don't see a contrived structure, which makes it very sophisticated."

Li's Reflection

"Exam" is a happy coincidence, in that not that all teachers agreed on what the paper was about, but they all liked what they thought the paper was about. For Mr. Wang and Mr. Zhang the message of the paper is obvious: "conquering self," as put by the Indian Saint in the most critical scene. Jack and Jane picked up the same scene, but came to a different interpretation: a critical scene in the process of making an important decision. For them it is a piece about making a mature and responsible decision. Yet no matter what their reading of the moral message, all four teachers thought the piece handled an important theme well.

Again, as with "Old Lady," both Jack and Jane find the opening and ending of "Exam" less than satisfying. What Mr. Zhang regards as the four essential components of all writing, "introduction, development, transition, and closure," are apparently not essential to the American teachers, who want the opening to put the reader directly on the scene and an ending that does not close up all possibilities. The word "introduction" is replaced by "lead," a journalistic term, in the talk of Jack and Jane. Introduction for the Chinese reader is like the Chinese custom of chatting over a cup of tea before the guests move to the dinner table, a leisurely custom incongruous with America's fast-paced life. American customers prefer to be led directly to the main course—and maybe have tea afterwards.

Subtlety is another important feature of good writing for Jack and Jane that they found "Exam" lacked. Subtle is antithetic to dramatization, which is seen almost as synonymous with contrivance. The word "subtle" occurred four times in Jack's comments on "Exam." He was dissatisfied with its ending because it is too explicit, too neat, erasing all ambivalence and doubts. As it happened with "Old Lady," such an ending was an awkward "moral tag" for Jane, "too neat" for Jack, but "a dragon's eye" for Mr. Wang and Mr. Zhang. There are two related questions to me: What is a good lead? What is the difference between an introduction and a lead? Why does an ending that states explicitly the moral lesson of the experience damage the credence of a piece? What is the difference between a message and a "moral tag"? Why is it so critical for a narrative to be subtle, inconclusive, instead of straightforward, just to tell a good story?

The following discussion focuses on these related questions.

Introduction and Lead

LI (*to Jane*): What is the difference between an introduction and a lead?

JANE: With an introduction the writer often thinks it is important to give the reader some background to get into it. The lead takes the reader right into it. The first thing that hit me in "Old Lady" was the small lane in summer, so we tend to scan until it drives in, if it drives in at all. It is hard to convince an inexperienced writer that they don't need to give us this background. What they do need to do is to decide whether they can involve us in the scene. Usually I ask them to read their piece silently and find the first line where something is really happening. And they will read that line aloud and I would say, why don't you start your piece there?

LI: But what's wrong with using the introduction to prepare the reader for what comes later?

JANE: But it doesn't say much yet. It doesn't start to say anything yet. This is an American thing, isn't it? I was trained in this: The opening should introduce you, lead you from the general to the specific, and the ending should summarize and conclude. But for the reader that has already happened. I tell students the writer owes the reader more than just restating in a different way or in the same way what they have already said. I ask them what you like as a reader, how effective it is to you as a reader. I ask them to think about something that can lead the reader. I told the class the other day, "It is like sitting in a car, if you slam the brakes on, the person goes flying forward, and that's where you leave the reader, in an unexpected position where they are still moving."

"Dragon's Eye" and "Moral Tag"

LI (*to Jane*): Let me ask you some questions about the conclusion. It seems to me you want the students to arrive at some universal ideas in their writing, but you also do not like generalizations at the end. How do they walk that line?

JANE: They make that universal leap when they begin to draw meanings for themselves. Many times, they are not thinking, and their writing gets so trite. When kids try to do the moral, it becomes corny and cliche, so they will say I learned from this, "ta-da!" That is what I try to keep them away from. If they add that moral tag, they blow the piece.

LI: What is the difference between a message and a moral tag?

JANE: A moral tag repeats what is established, but is meaningless to that individual.

LI: Some traditional morals still can be meaningful to the writer, can't they?

JANE: It can be, but these kids have been trained to look for a moral. It is a false attempt to make a statement, to make a generalization that really isn't necessarily true, and certainly not true for the reader for that particular piece of literature. Where in the piece did the old lady teach her sincerity? That ending is just added like a tag, not grown naturally out of it.

LI (*asking Jack*): You mentioned before that you believe that writing should have "a transcendent theme." How different is that from having a moral at the end?

JACK: A transcendent theme does not have to be serious; it could be just an amusing portrayal of life, jabbing at technology, for example. It's not moral. It's an observation of life.

We used to believe that literature presents a universal truth of human life. Well, you get into more contemporary literature, that view of literature is no longer valid. In recent years, particularly woman poets, like Ann Spencer, Adrienne Rich, will concentrate on the truth of woman's existence as to man's.

LI: Why did you say that the ending of "Exam" is too neat, too explicit?

JACK: It is also a cultural thing. I think Americans are much more likely to come to conclusions that allow for ambivalence and tentativeness, "Well, it may be right, it may be wrong. I don't know." I am so imbued in this culture that I find it hard to accept that this person is truly in her heart totally at peace with the decision and sure it was right.

LI: One reason why you like the piece "Grandpa" so much, as you told me, is because "It's subtle and suggestive." You like "Exam" when it is subtle and suggestive and like it less when it is too explicit. You seem to have a special predilection for subtlety. But as you said before, understanding is the purpose of writing. Won't the purpose of understanding be better served if the point of a paper is explicitly stated?

JACK: The means is as important as the end. For example, if I want to get my child to stop doing something, I could just tell him that it is forbidden. That might seem most effective, but there is no understanding of the other messages that go with it. I also want him to know it is for his own sake, as well as for mine. So the directness chews off all the other messages. If the message is subtle, it is richer, it takes all the innuendoes and clues and nuances that are going on right at that point. It holds them together.

And also it is more important for a reader to reach the conclusion for him or herself. This is the reader's ownership. Readers do not like to be told to think in certain ways. When a subtle approach is used, for instance, talking about capital punishment both at the emotional level and the psychological level, it causes the reader to search many levels of his reaction and come to a conclusion rather than keeping it at one level. Explicitness tends to force people to accept what is at one level.

THE "RIVER IN MY HOMETOWN" ("RIVER")

Teachers' Comments

MR. ZHANG: (Grade: 90.) Comments in chapter 1.

MR. WANG: (Grade: 86.) Written comments: "Clear organization, sharp contrast of the past and present. The whole piece reflects the change your hometown has gone through and your love for the river. It has very positive significance.

"The second paragraph is particularly vivid. The joy of the children is infectious. The third is also fine, but compared with the second paragraph it is not as specific. It seems much easier to write about one's own experience.

"The language flows well, and the choice of words is accurate, particularly the use of verbs, yet it is a bit too literary. It would be more appropriate if the language were less polished. Do you agree?"

In the margins, Mr. Wang complimented this sentence as using "concise language": "When winter was gone and spring came, the ice and snow melting, the earth waking up and seeds sprouting, the willow trees on the river bank showed green, and their branches danced with the spring breeze." The sentence in Chinese uses a string of four short phrases, each phrase consisting of four monosyllabic words, creating a very rhythmic effect.

JACK: (Grade: A-.) Written comments: "The image of a river linking all childhood experiences—the joy and the misery—into a single positive force for character growth is well established.

"The proverbs are woven skillfully into the text, also helping to establish the continuity of the river in the lives of all the people who live along it. Older generations have learned the same lessons and the future is built on the past.

"I am less sure of the use of pearls, because they are so positive an image, but that objection is minor. (The first paragraph could be omitted.)

"The other problem is an early reference to the river as 'paradise,' but several negative references to it come afterward. 'Paradise' is only about certain aspects of the river—certain times maybe.

"Skillful description. Clear focus on your point."

JANE: "I think the contrast works: 'However, the river in my hometown did not just flow with the kids' innocence and joy, it flowed with the misery and sorrow of our ancestors.' That's where the piece becomes poignant. Before that it [the river] stands alone; it does not do anything. The piece is an attempt to show something of his childhood, a little bit of the village, to show the parents did not live easy lives. But I can't believe the grandma was frozen to death and they waited at home. Do you believe that? 'Only Dad would sit on the river bank, mumbling.' I would ask the student if that is really true. [LI: Do you suspect it might be false?] No. As a matter of fact. It's a very moving piece: his reflection, the strong emotion for his father's anguish, his father's loss of not having seen what could become real. What is difficult in writing nonfiction is to write it as precisely and as emotionally effectively about the truth that the writer perceives.

"It is more difficult for me to be sure of honesty in a piece of writing from a Chinese student, whether the language they use indicates sincerity. [LI: This is written in a quite formal and very literary style, even poetic. Does that undermine its credibility?] I would not be able to find a student in my class who can write this formally and still be able to be very sincere. I am surprised that I am moved, because the formality could get in the way of the richness of the emotion. When it is contrived, you lose the poignancy of it, maybe the story itself, of the grandmother struggling to the river bank. I think it is a universal concept that our ancestors had it tough.

"The opening paragraph, I stopped a number of times, 'Life in childhood is like scattered pearls, bright and shiny, and the river in my hometown is a thread that strings together those pearls of joy and misery. . . .' There is too much in one sentence. But I like his attempt to create a metaphor and to use the river as a way to pull together these lives. But the pearl is not apt for images of joy and misery. I think the river works fine without the pearls.

"One of the things I look for in my students' writing is that they stay away from cliches and try to create a fresh way of looking at things. I had a difficult time to decide whether the student has written that or that's something that came out of the culture. I would point out some things that are good attempts at playing with the language. A sentence like 'the willow trees showed green' is not a cliche here. The language is nicely put together and the image is strong. Many of my students can't describe details, can't use the precise details that make something universal. For me, spring is the gold willow, that's the first thing I notice in spring, but they always talk about birds singing. I am not sure if 'river chuckles like silver bells' is cliche in your language. [LI: Not with rivers, usually with girls.] So he is playing with it. I like 'we sneaked out of our low-thatched houses' instead of just saying we sneaked out to the river bank. It's those details which begin to create a real place, a real home, a real life style and real people."

Li's Reflection

I am a bit surprised that "River" was better accepted by the American teachers than "Old Lady." Jack gave it an A-, compared with his B for "Old Lady." Jane, though having her moments of doubts, was moved by the piece despite its formal language and conventional structure—the image of the river appears both at the beginning and the end. The irony is that this piece, as Mr. Zhang admitted, does have elements of fiction after the revision. In the first draft, there were virtually no specifics of the the lives of the older generations, but some vague descriptions such as, "For years and generations, people on both sides of the river lived in low and yellow mud cottage. Here the earth was yellow, the cottages were yellow, as were the people's complexions and even their teeth." The most dramatic scenes in the story, the lonely death of the grandmother, the nearly demented father mumbling to himself after the death of his mother, were added (made up?) to underscore the theme, which, according to Mr. Zhang, is the contrast between the present society and the past to show the superiority of the new system. Jane is uncomfortable with some melodrama, but is less certain whether the piece is contrived.

Again, the piece was better received by Jack and Jane than "Old Lady," which was deemed the best by Mr. Wang and Mr. Zhang but graded low by Jane and Jack, because its theme has a universal appeal. As Jane pointed out, the idea that "our ancestors had it tough" is to her a "universal concept," although I assume what she had in mind was early American immigrants who, escaping political and religious persecution, braved the wilderness and other adversities, including the resistance of the native people, and settled in the new world. Mr. Wang and Mr. Zhang were revisiting a past of famine and utter poverty caused by a reactionary and corrupted government before the Communists took over, and the contrast between the old and the new system was what the writer was at pains to build.

The heavy use of proverbs, more than the two other Chinese pieces, fares well with Jack and Jane, too. The student, more out of luck than of good taste, did not write "lush green grass" or "singing birds" but "green willow trees," which is one of the most ancient images of spring and vitality in Chinese poetry. Just like centuries-old Chinese cuisine is a new addition to many American dinner tables, so "green willow trees" is a fresh image to the American readers. What is original and creative is relative to the audience.

Mr. Zhang calls both "Old Lady" and "River" lyrical prose *[san3 wen2]*, a genre somehow standing between poetry and prose and blending narrative with the writer's personal comments and sentiments on the topic. It has evolved from referring to anything that does not observe rhyme, meter, or other formal requirements of poetry to a very specific form of writing. Now the function of lyrical prose is basically expository rather than descriptive or narrative. It is short and does not tell a complete story; it foregrounds, instead, the writer's personal feelings and thinking provoked by some seemingly insignificant, sometimes scattered facts. The language of lyrical prose is very polished, literary, concise, and rich with historical references, poems, proverbs, and natural images.

All three Chinese pieces share a common feature: the frequent reference to something in the natural surroundings, which Jack referred to as "symbols" or "atmospherics" and which Jane called "imagery." In "Exam," it is the description of sunset and wild ducks, in "Old lady" the repeated mentioning of the trees, and in "River" the river and the signs of seasonal changes along the banks. In the discussion, Mr. Wang and Mr. Zhang referred to such rhetorical tropes as *"jing,"* literary translated as "scenery, exterior view," or, more loosely, "nature." The most accurate definition of *jing* is probably the most general: the opposite of the manmade world or objects. In the scheme of yingyang, it is the yang (heaven) as opposed to yin (human). Yet as the graphic of yingyang also demonstrates, the two spheres are intertwined and inseparable; man is part of *jing,* and *jing* is an extension of man. Jack observes, "She [author of "Exam"] chooses to begin two paragraphs with atmospherics rather than directly come back to her mind." But if all three pieces choose to do the same thing, it is more than an individual's choice. Rather, as Mr. Wang later points out, it is the claiming of a long and honored tradition in Chinese literature and ideology of man's position in the universe.

The Omnipresent Jing

LI (*to Mr. Wang*): Why is it that all three pieces, whether set in a small courtyard or along a city boulevard, whether about a next-door neighbor or the lives of one's ancestors, devote considerable space to the description of something in the natural surrounding?

MR. WANG: There are two most important artistic features of Chinese classic literature: one is the blending of *qing* (emotions) and *jing* (nature), and the other is its way of characterization.

Traditionally there are two ways to express one's *qing*: either directly express it, or indirectly through a description of nature. And because Chinese are mostly reserved and introverted in temperament, we prefer to "couch *qing* in *jing*," suggest what one feels through the description of nature. As Wang Guowei[10] generalized nicely, "All words of *jing* are words of *qing*, and all words of *qing* are also words of *jing*." So all descriptions of natural objects or scenery are for the sake of expressing emotions. This has been so throughout Chinese history of literature. In *The Book of Odes*[11] you can find plenty of poems that successfully blend the two. In one poem, when the soldier left home for war, it says, "Willow trees softly swaying," which expresses his love for his hometown and his reluctance to leave, yet when he returns only to find that his parents are gone, the poem goes, "sleet falling thick and fast." The change of weather conveys the emotional turmoil the soldier underwent when torn from his family in a war in a subtle and graceful manner. Chinese novels use the same technique. When Lin Cong[12] left for the mountain to join the rebels in *Waterside*, instead of directly describing how Lin Cong felt, it says, "the snow was swirling and howling," which more effectively shows the landscape of his mind at that moment.

Chinese ink painting is called "mountains-and-waters painting," and Chinese poetry is also often referred to as poems of mountains and waters. Nature provides inspiration as well as means of expression for artists. In the time of the Northern and Southern Dynasties, Liu Xie[13] said, "Ascending the mountain, the mountain is alive with *qing*; beholding the ocean, the ocean is brimming with *qing*." Wherever man looks, *jing* is colored with or colors man's *qing*. This view of nature in relation to man's emotion has been embraced by later generations. Now we still aspire toward the integration of *qing* and *jing*. And I believe such literary tradition is a treasure of our culture and should be carried forth to the future.

CONCLUSION

Jack, Jane, Mr. Wang, and Mr. Zhang are four unique individuals, each a complex and sometimes conflicting unity. Labels like "American writing teachers" or "Chinese writing teachers" can hardly tell who they are.

Jane is a staunch fighter against all forms of authority, which she believes have the undue consequence of stifling students' authentic "voices" and nullifying their sense of self. To nourish individualism free of all institutional bondage and trappings is the goal of her teaching. Her public iconoclasm, however, is at odds with her private life: a pious Christian seeking her own spiritual guidance from a religious establishment. Jack, a social and political conservative who even brings the Bible to a public school (only during off-hours, though), rebels against what he sees as "the liberal extremes running rampant" in America. He is much more receptive to tradition as a teacher, yet he is an avid practitioner of the "process" approach, letting the students take the center stage, and he enthusiastically embraces cultural pluralism. His aesthetic taste, a blend of realism and modernism, is as mixed as his values as a moderate conservative. As unflinching as he might be in denouncing social evils, Jack has a special proclivity for ambivalence and tentativeness in writing, even more so than Jane.

The same is true with the Chinese teachers. Mr. Wang supports the democratic demands of the Chinese students in Tiananmen Square and is hungry for new ideas from the West. His yearning for more personal freedom is being translated slowly into his everyday teaching. Compared with Mr. Zhang he prefers a more colloquial style in students' writing, yet he is not Jack or Jane. He is open to new ideas but he is still a Confucius scholar in the best sense of the term: a paragon of moral integrity. His evaluation of student papers clearly reflects his moralistic values. Mr. Zhang, an unabashed guardian of Chinese educational and literary traditions, is at the same time an outspoken critic of what he sees as the residue of the century-old "imperial examination." He insists most rigorously that student writing be measured, first and foremost, on the significance (the correctness?) of its ideological content, yet his nostalgia for a time in the early sixties when political control was more relaxed in China and students were able to write on anything reveals a different side of him. As Mr. Wang admitted regretfully, many teachers in China, for their own conscience and the safety of their students, had to teach students to draw a cautious line between what could be said in public and what should be kept only to oneself. The double standard, in fact, is not just some defense mechanism teachers in China pass on to their students, but what they have to abide by themselves. Mr. Zhang's single-minded insistence on ideological correctness is easier to understand when seen in that context.

Not surprisingly, there is by no means a clear-cut Chinese standard of "good writing" versus an American one. All four principal teachers were moved by the anguish and the painful sense of loss expressed in "To a Friend," and all were enchanted by the enigmatic Grandpa and his relationship with other family members. What Jack called "the atmospherics" in "Exam" and the thoughtful organization of "River" were well received by all four teachers. All teachers, maybe because they are teachers of language, were elated when they found student writers in good command of the language, capable of choosing apt and expressive terms to convey what they have seen or felt. Odd alliances sometimes took place between unexpected partners. Jack and Mr. Zhang, for example, despite their many differences, both had a soft spot for writing with good organization; what is "good," however, depends. Jack professed to have a special liking for a "clever" organization, and Mr. Zhang was far more specific: a piece threaded together with a recurring image, and the ending correlating with the beginning. Jane and Mr. Wang were more likely to fall for writing that has a strong emotional appeal, though for different reasons.

Although enough room should be granted to individuals' uniqueness, including their occasional lapses in judgment, one would have to ignore the obvious not to see the cultural divide among the four. If the four teachers can be placed on a spectrum from the most radical to the most conservative, for lack of better term (I wish I could strip these terms of their partisan connotations), the order is probably as such: Jane, Jack, Mr. Wang, and Mr. Zhang. Yet continuum is not the right concept here. There is a marked difference between Jane and Jack versus Mr. Wang and Mr. Zhang. The conservatism of Mr. Zhang is as different from that of Jack as the liberalism between Jane and Mr. Wang. The fact is that even though individuals may position themselves differently in respect to the prevailing ideology, unless they take a flight of fancy, individuals invariably operate within the parameters stipulated by the larger culture to which they both are subjected and contribute. The two parameters, overlapping in places and diverging at others, begin to emerge from the talks and comments by the four "principal" teachers. The following discussion highlights the places where the difference is most striking.

First of all, and most important, for Mr. Wang and Mr. Zhang writing is "a vehicle of *Tao*," the acquisition and dissemination of an honorable way of life that conforms to certain established moral codes. Good writing, therefore, should carry a positive or, more desirably, a profound moral message; never mind whether it be a mere reiteration of a popular witticism or what parents or teachers have preached to the writer. This is not only a recurring theme in Mr. Wang and Mr. Zhang's discussions and comments on specific papers, but is seen most clearly in the three selected pieces, "Exam," "Old Lady," and "River," each a showcase of that quality: "Exam" is a writer's confession of fighting selfish impulses, "Old Lady" is a paean of a selfless revolutionary veteran, and "River" an ode to the socialist system. Although Mr. Wang is less rigid than Mr. Zhang in this regard, their judgment is not far apart, if one looks at their independent—yet unanimous—high marks for "Old Lady" (86 from Mr. Wang, the second highest grade he gave to all the papers under discussion, and 100 from Mr. Zhang) in contrast to their lukewarm response to "Grandpa" (graded 82 and 75 respectively), even though they agreed that the author of "Grandpa" did an equally good, if not better, job of characterization. The source of their dissatisfaction with the latter was summed up by Mr. Zhang's response to the self-posed and answered rhetorical question in his commentary: "But what is the significance of presenting such a character and his story? Writing is for educating and molding people's minds."

Jack and Jane, by contrast, endeavor to stay away from moral judgment, facing what Jane called a "moral dilemma." Even Jack, despite his religious activism, prefers a piece that deals with "moral gray areas." "Grandpa" was highly praised by both of them for its depth and subtlety, and "Old Lady," on the other hand, criticized for adding an awkward "moral tag" by Jane and for lack of reflection by Jack. Jack gave the former an unqualified A and the latter a B, the lowest of all six pieces.

The primary function of writing for Jack and Jane is the exploration and expression of "self." As Jane expounded eloquently, "It is very important for writers to deal with life, to reflect, to look into themselves and the meaning of their lives. That's the whole purpose of writing as far as I am concerned." For that declared purpose, she takes some radical measures; she refuses to grade a student paper unless she knew the student personally, and she uses the conference, the more intimate form of communication, with her students to understand what the authors wanted to write and to avoid telling them what she wants them to write.

Repetition of a known moral dictum is to Jack and Jane slavishly following the convention at the expense of one's intellectual independence. One of the chief merits Jane saw in "To a Friend" was that it was written with authority, "saying things that no one else can say." With a hawk's vigilance, she hunted down signs of "contrivance" and "phony" posturing to safeguard a free and authentic persona of "self" in writing.

The two groups' widely divergent views on the primary function of writing underlie much of their other differences, setting them apart even at places where they seemed to converge. Both Jack and Mr. Wang in their talks showed an almost missionary zeal for students' spirituality, yet their evaluation of student papers revealed little in common in their actual practice. Jack, despite his deep concern with students' spiritual well-being, refrains from using teaching as a forum to offer spiritual guidance. Instead he views writing a journey without destination, the process of searching more important than where it ends. Reflection, observation, catharsis, posing questions, revealing complexities are worthy activities in and of themselves. He would rather the writer end a piece in ambivalence or ambiguity than settle for a facile or ready-made conclusion.

Mr. Wang, by comparison, although he asked his students to write about "a person who has a noble character and is worthy of our admiration and emulation," to discover "the real, the good, and the beautiful," never had any question in his mind as to what constituted "a noble character" and what was "worthy of admiration and emulation." What "the real, the good, and the beautiful" is has already been defined by moral authorities like Confucius and other saints before the writer came to the scene. Writing is a means through which the writer comes to terms with these well-established moral codes. Therefore, what the writer finds through writing is as important, if not more, as how she finds it; writing is a journey of confirmation rather than one of discovery that may end in suspense.

Secondly, the standards for form vary widely between the two groups. Mr. Wang and Mr. Zhang have no qualms setting specific requirements for forms: a piece of good writing should have a focus (concentrating on a few selected events or details that best illustrate the theme), a structural "thread" (preferably an image that connects all parts), and an opening that introduces the topic and an ending that correlates the opening, creating a sense of completeness.

Jack and Jane, on the other hand, seem to set few formal standards other than focus (having a central theme, which is often implied rather than explicitly stated). Because, as Jane explained, she would like her students to learn "to make choices not following a format handed down from the teacher," therefore as a teacher she acts like a reader, asking "questions as a reader would, rather than giving answers." Given their different perception of their role as teachers and their different expectations in terms of structure, both Mr. Zhang and Mr. Wang found "Summer Camp" falling far short of good writing, giving it the lowest grades (61 from Mr. Zhang and 83 from Mr. Wang, one point higher than what he gave to "Grandpa"). They both considered the piece "disorganized," not having a structural "thread," not focusing on a few most memorable events or details, and just trailing off at the end. Interestingly enough, structure was the very merit for which Jane commended the piece: for the first time, she emphasized, the writer was able to "let writing happen without trying to formalize it." Whatever reservation Jack had about "Summer," it is not with its structure. In fact, he pronounced that its structure is "very good," and that he had "no problem at all." Such free flow, a chronological flow, I would say, but disparaged by Mr. Zhang as "drifting," is just fine with Jack and Jane.

"Old Lady," on the other hand, the best of the six pieces by Mr. Wang and Mr. Zhang's standard, was criticized most severely by Jane precisely because of the kind of form that Mr. Wang and Mr. Zhang seek to implant in student writing. She considered the writer's deliberate contrast of the protagonist with a fat man "a contrivance," and found the same image at the beginning and at the end to be an imitation of "a kind of formalized standard framework." The whole piece, as a result, appeared "phony" in her judgment.

But it would be a gross misrepresentation to conclude that Jack and Jane do not care about the form. Both of them were very stringent in the way in which a piece starts, whether the opening qualifies for a good "lead," which, according to Jack, differs from an "introduction" in that it takes the reader right into the center of the action rather than preparing the reader for it. In that regard they found all three pieces written by Chinese students lacking.

Thirdly, the line between the written and the oral is purposely blurred in Jack and Jane's comments—the use of "voice" instead of style is one of the outcomes. In keeping with their belief that good writing should demonstrate the writer's unique perspective on life, Jack and Jane stress that good writing should have the distinct voice of the writer, employing a language that is "natural," which to my understanding means less crafted and polished, verging on, if not resembling, the colloquial. To achieve that, Jane often spends weeks getting her students to write "fast and furiously, so that they can't rework to make it sound good." The bias towards the more colloquial, which is synonymous with more "natural," is most clearly seen in the evaluation of "To a Friend." Jack gave it a relatively high grade of "B+," for "it sounds like the kid," although, in his judgment, the piece was "not as nicely crafted and polished."

The two teachers, however, did not always agree on what was "natural." "Summer Camp" was, according to Jack, a deliberate attempt by the writer to "move far away from his natural voice, to want to sound like a writer." Therefore he deemed the piece too literary to such as extent that it sounded "phony." Yet what was "too literary" for Jack was "very natural" to Jane, who considered that "Summer Camp" represented one of the rare occasions when students did not use cliches and "found language uniquely their own."

Mr. Zhang and Mr. Wang did not always see eye to eye on what was "too literary" either. "River," recommended by Mr. Zhang for its exemplary showing of "literary grace," was "a bit too literary" for Mr. Wang. Yet the notion that students should find their unique voice in their writing seemed an alien notion to both of them, for never once did they consider a piece "phony" for its use of ornate or overly dramatic language, nor did they expect the colloquialization of the written language. If they had to decide on a model that represents good writing, Mr. Wang and Mr. Zhang would probably choose one that resembles poetry, which, as Jack rightly pointed out, is a highly contrived form of writing. The two Chinese teachers each independently focused and lavished compliments on the scene at the dock at sunset in "Summer Camp" as the part most beautifully written, despite their disapproval for the "flat and dull" organization of the entire piece. All three pieces by the Chinese students demonstrate features of what Mr. Zhang calls "lyrical prose": natural images, symbols, succinct and literary diction, highly selective details, and, more importantly, the blending of *qing* (emotion) and *jing* (scenery).

Finally, if poetry is the model of good writing for Mr. Wang and Mr. Zhang, science seems to be the model at the back of Jack and Jane's mind, even though the term "science" never once passed their lips. That may partly explain their fixture on "honesty" in their evaluations. Their relentless scrutiny of honesty in students' writing smacks of scientists' endeavor for truth, the result of which is assessed less in terms of beauty than of logic and truthfulness.

Jane quickly pointed out that the claim of the writer at the end of "Old Lady" that the old lady taught her to be sincere was not consistent with the piece, for although the old lady was kind and modest, nothing in the piece portrayed her as particularly sincere. She also questioned the probability of grandma freezing to death alone in the winter in "River." One reason why Jane is adamantly against "moral tags" is, as she told us, that such tags are generalizations (the finding) not based on the writer's actual experience (the data) but conveniently grafted from popular cliches (outdated theories). That, of course, is bad science. Just as bad is when truthfulness and accuracy are shortchanged for high drama, which is what Jane suspected what the writer was attempting when she introduced the fat man into the story at the end of "Old Lady."

Jack's peculiar taste for subtlety and ambivalence, on the other hand, is not all that different from that of a cautious scientist faced with a complex and perplexing phenomenon, unwilling to draw conclusions based on scanty data. He also dissects student papers with the precision of a surgeon's scalpel. He objected to the use of "paradise" in "River," for it is not an apt image for a river that was a site for both joy and misery. He also pointed out the logical flaw in the image of the "pearls" in the opening paragraph, a positive image used for mixed memories of innocence, joy, and sorrow. Jane, incidentally, made the similar observation in regard to the image of the pearls.

All these inconsistencies and flawed logic were glossed over by Mr. Wang and Mr. Zhang, for a reason. Mr. Zhang, in response to the question of honesty, states, "As long as the artistic creation is not far removed from what could actually happen in real life and does not violate commonsense logic, it is in line with Marxist Realism." His commonsense logic is obviously one much more lenient one than that followed by his American counterparts, and Marxist Realism is not the same as American Realism. But most importantly, writing is seen by Mr. Wang and Mr. Zhang as artistic creation entitled to poetic license that allows for occasional logical lapses and even factual concoctions.

There are other less significant differences I have not included here. But it is safe to conclude that, from the student writings the two groups selected and their frank discussions, Mr. Wang and Mr. Zhang think better of pieces that convey clear and positive moral messages and demonstrate a good mastery of conventional forms and the features of Chinese poetry. Jack and Jane, on the other hand, prefer writing that impresses them as "unique," demonstrating the writer's intellectual rigor and originality. The irony is: while Jack and Jane genuinely encourage students to depart from rutted tracks, they enforce new standards, though few in number, just as rigorously.

These diverse aesthetic and rhetorical criteria explain in part why the same piece scored very differently with the two groups of teachers. What was outstanding for Jack and Jane could be just average for Mr. Wang and Mr. Zhang, as with "Grandpa" what was perfect for Mr. Wang and Mr. Zhang, likewise, as in the case of "Old Lady," was viewed problematic by Jack and Jane. There are no universal criteria; what is beautiful is decided by who the beholder is.

Listening to the two groups of teachers, I was struck by the manner in which each group related to the past. Time seemed to be compressed into a small capsule when Mr. Wang and Mr. Zhang talked. Ideas and words put forth thousands of years ago were quoted frequently and directly from memory as if they came out only yesterday. The authority of Confucius, Mencius, and other classic authors who wrote centuries ago had not diminished with the lapse of time, and their names and works still held such persuasive power that they were cited to buttress up or explain their present practice and thinking. Jack and Jane, on the other hand, seldom quoted from anybody in their talks. When asked for the sources of their teaching philosophies, Jack referred to his own experience as a writer and Jane to her disillusionment with the educational system in America. When they talked about the past, as when Jack did about Archibald MacLeish's popularity in his school days and Jane about the sixties, it was used to illustrate the changes that have happened in the course of the time and the consequences of such changes. The past has lost its aura of authority on them.

Their perception of their relationship with the past, it seems to me, has direct consequences on the ways in which they teach and evaluate student writing. Mr. Wang and Mr. Zhang perceive of themselves as and act like a link between the past and students to form an unbroken chain that stretches as far back as three thousand years. To achieve that they offer clear guidance when students stray from the right track; they are eager to demonstrate to students the right way. (They both supplied titles to the papers whose titles are missing, and grade their papers based on how well the writer has mastered the ancient craft of writing.)

Jack and Jane, on the other hand, bend towards change, novelty, and originality, viewing the free, uncontaminated, authentic "self" to be students' treasured asset. "Be yourself. Be different, as long as you follow the ground rules of logic and truthfulness," they seem to say to their students. They may raise questions, urge the student to probe other possibilities, or simply cheer for good work and point out the shortfalls, but they refrain from feeding students answers and solutions. Individuals should find their places in the world on their own, and of their own volition. Maybe that is the essence of democracy.

CHAPTER 3

Forty-Five Teachers and Four Pieces

Are the four principal teachers' criteria for good writing representative of writing teachers in the two countries? Is it possible that the cultural divide seen between them is only an accident or a coincidence? To answer those questions, a survey was conducted among sixty teachers, thirty in each country. The survey, however, is too modest in scope to draw a final checklist for "good" writing, but should be enough to bolster the proposition that good writing is culturally and historically constructed. If two parameters, tentative as they were, emerged from the discussion and dialogue among the four principal teachers, the sixty teachers' evaluations should help delineate the their outlines further.

For a better return, I reduced the number of student writings from six pieces to four. "Beat Them 'til They're Black and Blue," "There was an Old Lady," "Untitled 1 (To a Friend)," and "Me, Before and After the Exam" were selected and sent to thirty teachers in each country for their comments.

The respondents were not asked to grade the papers, not only because of the two different grading systems—the hundred-mark versus the five-letter—used in the two countries, but because grades, as I found earlier in the study, had little comparative value even within the same system. Mr. Wang said that he rarely delivered 90 and almost never gave 95, and his grade of 86 for "Old Lady" was a very good grade. Mr. Zhang was much more generous with grades; therefore, his grade of 100 for "Old Lady" should probably be read as Mr. Wang's "90." But experienced teachers are fairly consistent with their own grading. So in the survey, instead of grades, I asked the respondents to rank the four pieces in order. The American respondents were asked to assume that they were serving on an advisory board to a student magazine and the Chinese respondents on a committee that judges the outcome of a composition contest. Whatever their capacity, their job was the same: to rank the four pieces of writing submitted by the students and explain their decisions in terms of the strengths and weaknesses of each piece. The audience for the comments would be the other teachers on the same board or committee rather than the student authors. Twenty-three (76.7 percent) valid responses from

China and twenty-two (73.3 percent) from America were returned, which indicates tremendous interest in and support for such a study in both countries. Tables 3.1 and 3.2 summarize the result.

The most noticeable discrepancy between the four principal teachers and the result of the survey is the evaluation of "To a Friend," a piece well received by all four principal teachers (both Mr. Wang and Mr. Zhang gave it a higher grade than "Grandpa," while Jack and Jane graded it higher than "Old Lady"). It sinks to the last in the survey. There are teachers in both countries who share their reading (two respondents from America rank it the best, and four from China rank it the second best), but they are clearly the minority. On the whole, however, it is safe to say that the four principal teachers' readings are consistent with those of their colleagues in their country. They may occasionally swerve slightly from the course, but their evaluation is by no means atypical.

Surveys of such a limited scope can only give us an incomplete glimpse at tendency, yet the glimpse here is quite revealing. There is surprising consensus among American respondents: the majority of the twenty-two American respondents rank "Grandfather" as the best (64 percent of the respondents), "Old Lady" the second best (55 percent), "Exam" in third place (59 percent), and "To a Friend" last (68 percent). There is, however, little consensus among the Chinese respondents other

Table 3.1
American Respondents (Total: 22)

Rank	1	2	3	4
"Grandfather"	14 (64%)	6 (27%)	1 (6%)	1 (4.5%)
"Old Lady"	6 (27%)	12 (55%)	4 (18%)	
"Exam"	1 (5%)	2 (9%)	13 (59%)	6 (27%)
"To a Friend"	2 (9%)	1 (5%)	4 (18%)	15 (68%)

Table 3.2
Chinese Respondents (Total: 23)

Rank	1	2	3	4
"Grandfather"	9 (39%)	8 (35%)	2 (9%)	4 (17%)
"Old Lady"	12 (52%)	5 (22%)	6 (26%)	
"Exam"	2 (9%)	6 (26%)	7 (30%)	8 (35%)
"To a Friend"		4 (17%)	8 (35%)	11 (48%)

than that the majority rank "Old Lady" as the best (52 percent). It is ironic that from the first round of discussion I concluded that American teachers embrace change while the Chinese teachers hold on to continuity, yet the survey seems to indicate the opposite: there is a greater degree of disagreement among the Chinese teachers than among their American counterparts. It seems that as China is undergoing radical changes politically and economically, so the teachers of writing in China are undergoing the same kind of disorientation, confusion, transformation, and flux that any social change of this magnitude would cause. On the other hand, although American teachers like to think of themselves as free agents, unbound by institutional constraints, they demonstrate more uniformity than their Chinese counterparts. Can the uniformity in their rating suggest some kind of conformity despite their alleged independence?

Numbers hardly tell the whole truth. It is in the teachers' commentary that the four principal teachers' voices are loudly confirmed, amplified, or deflected. Although "To a Friend," for example, is ranked last by both the American and the Chinese respondents, the reason behind their identical judgment could not be more different.

The teachers were asked to evaluate each essay as they would one written for them by a student from their country (but withhold their judgment of grammar, spelling, punctuation, or penmanship, features lost in translation), yet I was concerned, when sending out the survey, that the American respondents, in a time of multiculturalism to be non-ethnocentric, would bend over to be nice to the Chinese pieces and the Chinese respondents, eager to adopt Western values in the current climate of modernization in China, might be too easy on the American pieces. While such considerations cannot, and should not, be ruled out, the result of the survey shows that most participants were refreshingly candid, and some mercilessly frank. There were even a few, aware that the study was cross-cultural, who suggested what the rating might be if the essay were read with a different mindset and criteria.

As the discussions among the four teachers also demonstrate, there is a full range of opinions within each country, defying any attempts to reduce the situation to two monolithic camps. The following is a sample of the multifarious comments from both countries on each of the four essays.

"GRANDFATHER"

"Grandfather" outranks the rest, according to most American respondents, because of its "excellent narrative style." Twenty American respondents state in their comments, in one way or another, that the most outstanding characteristic of the paper, is that it "shows more, tells less." As one teacher remarks, "[It has] more fully developed descriptions than others (more showing, more physical details)." They like its use of "sensory," "appropriate," "concrete," and "well-chosen" details, and "vivid," "wonderful," "evoking," "strong," as well as some "contrasting" images, such as the lingering smell of the pipe and the switching whip. All these give them "a good feel of the man" and "a feel of the tension as well as the beauty of the memory." The piece has a distinctive individual voice, because "It sounds like the particular experience of an individual."

A number of American respondents compliment the paper as having "depth" or being "perceptive" or "sensitive"; one of them remarks, "This is a good beginning to character examination and a look into a vital human relationship as well as the lack of one." Others like its "fluid" sentence structure and "vivid, effective choice of words," and praise its overall organization as "focused," "controlled and coherent," or having "movement and shape." The title and the opening also impress a number of respondents.

Yet almost half of the American respondents (eleven) are dissatisfied with the development of the relationship between the mother and grandfather. One of them points out, "Too many questions left unanswered"; and another comments, "Deeper awareness and make-believe stories incomplete, underdeveloped, points toward something important, then doesn't go there." Yet some of them acknowledge, at the same time, the evocative power of such ambiguity. As one teacher remarks, "The relationship between the grandfather and his daughter [is] not explored sufficiently, but there is real power and possibility in what is unsaid."

Many Chinese respondents join in the accolade with their American colleagues, but almost unanimously they read it as a successful personal profile; few heed the more universal aspect of the piece: the revelation of human relationship between generations. They praise the portrayal of the grandfather as "sharp," "strong," "well-developed," and "hard to understand but hard to forget." They are particularly impressed with the "vivid" and "minute" description of the grandfather's physical appearance at the beginning. Most of them view the successful characterization a result of the writer's skillful selection and arrangement of the details, creating an unexpected effect. Most comments, therefore, are directed at the writer's skill of organization; some take pains to analyze its plot and organization. One teacher's observation is quite typical of their analysis: "The author weaves together the conflicting anecdotes of the grandfather, convincingly portraying an extremely ordinary, unsophisticated farmer with a strong personality. As a father to his children, he is extremely rigid and severe (close to cruel); yet as a grandfather to his grandchild, he is extremely kind and loving." Another teacher finds the same quality in the paper: "Cold and severe, but also caring and loving, he was strained by the burden of raising six daughters but enchanted by his only granddaughter. With the display of the contrasting facets of the grandfather, the story is profound and soul-stirring." A few teachers also like what they call the "suspense" of the story, one comparing the somehow mysterious father-daughter relationship to the creation of blank spaces in Chinese painting, with the effect of "leaving ample room for the reader's imagination."

Quite a number of Chinese readers, however, find the "blank space" perplexing rather than evocative. One teacher, who ranked the piece fourth, asks: "Why is it that the grandfather was unable to love his own daughters? Was it because of hardship, poverty, or some other reason? What is the implication of the title 'Beat Them 'til They're Black and Blue'? The paper expresses only the writer's impressions of a family situation without realizing the puzzlement in which it leaves the reader. The writer is not thinking of the reader, writing only for self-expression." Three other teachers fault it as "unfocused," "straying from the subject." An equal number of teachers who rank the paper second and third point to the "lack of clarity" as the major problem of the paper, and the lack of a significant message. One of them, who likes the mystery of the story, ends his comments with the remark, "The piece eventually loses [its first place] for its subject matter; it portrays an unfathomable, strange old man, which does not have the same significance as 'There is an Old Lady.'" His view, however, is not shared by some teachers who read a different message from the piece. They suggest that "Grandfather" is a worthy piece that expresses the theme of "love," and the title implies "a philosophy of life that advocates determination and fight."

To sum up, the responses from both countries are quite similar to those of the four key teachers. The piece wins the hearts of the American respondents for its narrative style, the writer's ability "to show and not to tell," and its perceptive examination of human relationship. It fascinates the Chinese readers, on the other hand, for its "thoughtful and clever conception" of the story, and its selection of the most revealing details to show the conflicting facets of a complicated character. Although a substantial number of respondents in both countries want fuller development of the relationship between the grandfather and the mother, this problem does not affect more than half of the American teachers' high evaluation of the piece, whereas Chinese teachers, on the whole, take it as a more serious structural flaw, and most of them do not consider this the best of the four pieces. In addition, some Chinese teachers think the piece does not say anything "really meaningful," a criticism not shared by any American readers.

"OLD LADY"

Just as most American respondents feel most pleased with "Grandfather" for its narrative style, most Chinese respondents find "Old Lady" coming closest to their ideal texts for both its style and content. One teacher puts it plainly: "'There is Such an Old Lady' is the best of the four, which means, compared with the rest, it best suits my taste. It conforms to the standard. The style is fresh and lively, the organization thoughtful and skillful; it has a sharp theme that entertains lofty ideas. Based on these merits, it deserves the highest position."

Most Chinese teachers (fifteen) agree with his evaluation of its style and structure, particularly features like "the beginning and the end echo each other," "the story unfolds like taking off layer after layer of a bamboo shoot," "[it] uses contrast, personification, metaphors, suspense, and other direct and indirect means of expression." The symbolic meanings of the trees and flowers are accorded their special attention. One teacher remarks, "The anecdote of the old lady planting trees, as if dropped in casually, adds a critical comment and development to the character." Some teachers like the conclusion of the paper, saying that "it brings the theme to a new height," or "the brief comments reveal the central theme of the paper." No one finds fault with the added trait of "sincerity" in the last line.

Yet a significant number of teachers (five) find the structure "too conventional" and "too jaded." One of them elaborates, "The so-called 'disposition' of the old lady, her 'thin' and 'straight' back, as well as that 'fat man' and the writer's revisit to the lane after ten years, all these are quite delicious when first read but tasted stale when chewed over." The teacher who made this remark ranked the paper third.

Overwhelmingly, though, the positive theme of the piece overrides its shortcomings. Sixteen other Chinese respondents commended the theme of the piece, as one of them comments, "The young writer portrays a kind, modest, and sincere lady, which enables the reader to experience the broad mind of this veteran revolutionary and her rich and deep emotions. It is an ode to lofty humanity and a call for sincerity. The contrast between the old lady and the 'fat man' clearly reveals the intent and affinities of the writer. . . . The outstanding characteristic of the piece is its in-depth reflection of reality. It also handles narration and description skillfully. Therefore, of the four pieces, this is the best."

The subject matter and the moral significance of the paper, however, are not major concerns for most American respondents; only a few commented on that aspect of the paper, one describing it as "a fine show of praise for a worthy person to be celebrated," and another remarking that "It says something significant: that action rather than looks are what make heroes." Some want the writer to explore her own mind deeper, and one of them asks directly, "What did you learn about yourself?"

A good number of American readers' interest is captured by the conversation between the old lady and the child, as one of them comments: "There is some small charm in the naive and unsophisticated view and interpretation of the narrator." Still another comments that "The conversational style works well. The narrator has an individual voice," which is a rare compliment for Chinese writing.

Another feature that arouses great interest among the Americans is the use of "the details in the setting" (some call them "images"), read as having symbolic or metaphorical implications. With relish, one teacher interprets the symbolic meaning of every detail that he sees as having an implied reference. He not only sees the obvious connection between the parasol trees and the old lady, but also the violet flowers that overgrew her wall and spread into the lane as suggesting the influence of the old lady, the seeds as the gift of legacy, and the demolition of the house as "her memory surviving with the trees. It is as if this lady can be removed, but her influence will live on."

A number of respondents comment positively on the essay's overall organization or some aspects of it. One of them observes, "well- shaped piece; it has a clear structure and evolves to a clear resolution"; another, "It has a finished feel to it. It is focused, balanced in terms of scene, fairly well-developed and complete, although the ending is not as strong as it might be."

Seven teachers agree with his last line; as one of them puts it, "I wish the author had allowed the image of the trees to 'show' the reader what the current final line 'tells' the reader." Five of them, a telling number compared with none of their Chinese counterparts, detected the flawed use of "sincerity" in the last line: "Why end with sincerity when we don't see this trait developed throughout?" Some teachers also find the beginning and the title ineffective.

Although some American teachers are satisfied with the description of the old lady and the selection of details, a significant number of teachers (six) think that it tells too much. One respondent comments, "The fact that the woman represents strength, inspiration, and sincerity, those traits need to be shown through what the old woman does and says; instead we are told straight out." Another respondent has the same reaction: "It suffers from the thinness of the description of the encounters on which the ending is based." One teacher considers it a matter of pace: "It tries to cover too much ground—moves too fast; at its best when it slows down, describes."

"That fat man episode" evokes the same negative reaction from some of the respondents as it did from Jane. One teacher comments, "This [the fat man] is to contrast, but it seems contrived." Another respondent does not like it either: "The fat man and his bragging are a bit too obvious a contrast; the point can come clear without him."

In short, "Old Lady" endears most Chinese respondents, for its didactic message through the portrayal of an admirable revolutionary, its well-conceived structure, and the use of various rhetorical devices and organizational techniques, except for a few teachers who consider it "too conventional." It is not the favorite piece of most American respondents because it could have "told" less, especially in the ending, which is too straightforward and superfluous for most of them. Quite a number of them like especially its use of symbolic images and "the finished feel" of the story, though.

The result from the Chinese respondents, most of whom place it indisputably in the first place, confirms Mr. Wang and Mr. Zhang's exceptionally high grading of the piece. The response from the American teachers, the majority of whom rank it second, is more positive than that of Jack and Jane, although their analyses of the piece are amazingly similar to those given by Jack and Jane.

"EXAM"

Compared with "Old Lady," a much smaller number of Chinese teachers (eight) are impressed by the theme of "Exam," which is interpreted as "conquering self" by most and "love for nature" by two. At the same time, a significant number of teachers (five) question the import of the paper. As one of them comments, "That the writer gave up a composition contest in order to take part in an ornithology test is inappropriate. First of all, the writer ignores the concern of the teacher, the sound advice of her classmate, which shows her insensitivity to others' feelings; secondly, she refuses to work for the honor of the collective; and, finally, to make a decision that indulges a personal hobby is a show of selfishness."

Three teachers, who rank the piece at the bottom of the whole set, go further and question the credence of the piece. One of them remarks, "It should be pointed out that the events narrated and emotions expressed in the piece are not necessarily true. If the teacher did not know there was conflict in schedule between two exams, the student should have reported it to the teacher, especially after the teacher had spent several lunch breaks to tutor her, yet the student did not even give her any hint." The ground on which they question the credence of the piece is clearly the readers' sensitivity to proper teacher-student relationship in China rather than the style of the piece.

An overwhelming number of teachers (twenty) are impressed by the descriptions of nature (*jing*), of the internal world of the narrator (*qing*), and the blending of the two. One teacher observes, "The piece describes and reveals with delicacy and vividness the conflicting and complex psychology of 'I' before and after the exam. It is especially worth mentioning that to depict that process, the writer employs not just internal monologues, but projects her feelings onto the natural scenery, transforming *jing yu* (the words of nature) to *qing yu* (the words of emotions)."

Yet quite a number of teachers (six) find that the essay leaves much to be desired in its description of nature. Some point to the repetition, and some think the natural scene alone does not provide convincing reasons for the final decision. Two teachers think the elements of description, comments, and the expression of emotions in the piece are not woven in organically.

Eight teachers like the piece because it is "natural," "real," and "moving." As one of them acclaims, "Its most outstanding characteristic is that it reflects the real psychological state of a high school student through depicting the complex mental change of 'I' from hesitation and self-doubt before the exam to joy and relief after the exam. . . . The process is written naturally, fluidly, accurately, emotionally, and excitingly. This is the main reason why the piece can move the reader." He ranked the piece second. Another teacher had a similar response: "The writer shows carefully the care and the hope of the teacher for her, and just because of that, the decision was a very difficult one. It intensifies the internal conflicts experienced by the writer and leads to the process, after which the writer finally overcame the hesitation and made the right decision. It is real and believable."

Actually there is neither severe criticism of its organization and style nor any indication of great excitement. The comments on the piece are generally brief compared with other pieces. Only five teachers mention features other than the blending of nature and emotions, such as its being "complete," its having "clear layers of development," and the use of "flashbacks."

The comments by the American respondents on this piece are more elaborate, although they are also more negative than positive.

There is somehow more enthusiasm about the subject matter of this piece than about "Old Lady," yet the Chinese interpretation of the theme, "conquering self," again totally eludes the American readers, who read it as either "maturing through making difficult decisions" or "the love and commitment to nature." As one teachers puts it, "It could become a strong piece, because it has a potentially powerful theme—the deeper meaning of attachment to nature than of personal triumph." Not one American reader, however, questioned the writer's decision to give up the composition exam, as a good number of Chinese readers did; there is only approval and praise. It seems that for American readers, whether or not such a decision would hurt the feelings of people concerned and "the honor of the collective" is not as important as the ability to make an independent decision.

A great number of American respondents, however, as are their Chinese colleagues, are enchanted by the connection between the description of nature and that of the mind of the narrator. One of them exclaims, "Really good! Metaphor to the free-flying ducks is skillfully transferred to the student and exam." Another teacher has a similar reaction: "Much of the writing here is strong, especially the last page and a half. It is vivid and I can see the speaker's transition in attitude through the natural images. The ducks and birds flying into the sun are powerful, moving pictures."

One teacher sums up her appreciation of the two Chinese pieces in this way: "The two Chinese students' pieces are delicate in feeling and thought and imagery—the courage and interest in creating metaphor and using dialogue is delightful—the writing has depth and credence."

But such compliments are rare amidst a storm of critical responses. Irritated and confused, one teacher responds, "The piece is extremely irritating in its omissions. I find half the events of the story confusing: why is the student placed in this position in the first place? What is the implication of the mother's advice about conquering oneself? (The problem seems to be external rather than internal to the writer.) Why does an ornithology test symbolize a life of commitment to the preservation of habitats and species? Why are the description of the birds so general?" A number of other teachers share his bewilderment; one of them writes, "I have trouble with the logic of the story. . . . It is hard to understand why 'conquering the self' amounts to failing to follow through on the commitment to the contest for which the teacher had helped the speaker to prepare. This is a division between content and form. The writing is quite strong. The logic issue undermines the vivid prose."

For others, however, the style of the piece is just as questionable. One respondent remarks, "A descriptive passage [is] never allowed to develop as sense-appeal passages—always forced into something with a conclusion." Another teacher has the same observation: "Some precise and vivid details combined with cliche and overblown statements." Still another: "tells, doesn't show—the reader wants to be actively involved rather than spoon-fed."

For some teachers the question of style calls into question the credence of the piece. One of them remarks, "The various components in the story are pretty well established. . . . But the presentation of all these components is heavy-handed, and I end up not 'believing' the story emotionally, however much I may approve intellectually of its outcome. In a word, the story doesn't engage me very much; like its title, it is too straightforward and maybe obvious." Another respondent is more blunt: "I don't believe the character's dilemma for one minute; I can't believe that Miss Lee wasn't consulted, her mother had only a quotation for her, etc. All of the characters are flat, they have no flesh and blood or minds. This is a very unsophisticated piece of writing that seems to take some second-rate eighteenth- or nineteenth-century prose as model."

On the whole, what is perceived as melodrama and sentimentality is the major reason why this piece received such negative responses from most American readers. One reader describes it as "pathetic, sentimental," another calls it "overdramatic," and still another describes it as having "that studied, artificial feel to it," saying that "this is a story told as if by rote."

The conclusion evokes a negative reaction just as strongly. One teacher suggests, "I think the writer would have done better to show us the birds, the sunset—without telling us it was important and beautiful—we know that already. . . .Cutting out the cliches and unnecessary explanations would make this piece sharper, more intense." The title and the introduction are considered by a number of teachers as "weak," too.

To conclude, "Exam" lags distantly far behind "Old Lady" when judged by American readers, many of whom are offended by its "sentimental" and "overdramatic" plot and curt and "heavy-handed" style. This is, at least, a mild surprise, since in the last round of discussion Jack and Jane responded more favorably to it than to "Old Lady." But among the Chinese readers the result of the survey is fairly consistent with Mr. Wang and Mr. Zhang's evaluation of the piece, both of whom liked the piece for its weaving of *"qing"* and *"jing"* but gave it a lower mark than "Old Lady," because its *liyi* (thematic significance) and organization are not on the same par.

"TO A FRIEND"

There are two things in "To a Friend" that most American respondents focus on as praiseworthy: the strong emotion and the introductory sentences. One teacher expresses the gut-level reaction of most teachers: "On a personal level, this piece is moving, because the pain is so palpable." And two teachers believe the piece has it own function; as one of them remarks, "It undoubtedly proved therapeutic to the author."

But it is because of those features that the same teachers find it too private, too crude, and even "phony." One of them has this to say about the piece: "This unshaped, unsophisticated cry of grief belongs to a diary." Another has the same paradoxical response: "while I want to feel strongly about what happened, and I think I ought to feel strongly about what happened, I just don't." Surprisingly, some teachers find the piece "filled with cliches," something Jane worked so hard with the student to avoid. A number of teachers think the piece suffers from the lack of emotional control. One of them comments, "Uncontrolled, almost peevish. Essentially a gush"; and another, "I suspect that the events of the story are true and too emotionally raw for the author to spend time filling in the physical detail." Other teachers have the same reaction, and one of them remarks, "raw emotions, unedited, unrevised"; and another, "sincerity becomes sentimentality."

The lack of details and specifics sharply brings down the estimation of the piece by a good number of teachers (ten). One critiques, "Too much statement of emotion and idea, too little specific detail and restraint, I always have trouble with such writing." Some others observe, "Too vague, needs more specific details to illustrate feeling," and "no sensory detail—or very little."

Five teachers question the credence of the piece because of the lack of specifics. One of them remarks, "I suspect she never had the experience." Another shows a similar reaction: "Pretty bland, vague, and uninteresting, too many empty rhetorical questions, finally because we don't learn much about either person or their relationship, we are unmoved. . . . I feel nothing for the speaker and don't believe that s/he was confused, angry, etc." Another teacher does not go that far, but comments, "No clear picture, doesn't show, could have been written by anyone."

A significant number of Chinese respondents share the criticisms of their American colleagues that the piece is lacking in craft and good details. Four teachers, for instance, think the simple outpouring of emotions does not give the piece enough substance; three others think the piece is not well organized and clearly expressed. Yet few question its credence. On the contrary, there is a surge of compliments for what they perceive as "honest, strong, and sincere emotions." The strong reaction to the emotional force of the piece is eloquently expressed by the following two Chinese respondents, whose feelings are shared by nineteen others. One writes: "The composition expresses the author's sorrow for the inconsequential death of her friend. It is written straight from the heart, sincere and intense, painfully moving. She addresses her friend directly as if she were alive and blames her for abandoning their friendship. There are also affectionate memories along with regrets and self-reproach for her own delayed understanding. Finally she offers her hearty prayers for her friend. It reveals her agony and other emotions in one wave after another, lapping at the heart of the reader. These are done very effectively." The other also admits his submission to its emotional power: "It expresses forcibly the author's sincere, faithful love and unadulterated affection for her friend (or lover). It is hard to hold back tears when reading. . . . 'Writing is valued for its honesty.' A high school student who can produce such an honest piece is exceptional." The unusual use of the second person in the piece and its effective use of rhetorical questions also wins approval from a number of Chinese teachers.

Nine Chinese teachers, however, find the thematic import of the piece problematic. The same teacher who considers the writer "exceptional" questions, "Should a high school student be allowed to write a piece like this? Does it have any positive and immediate significance? I think these questions are worth pondering." Another teacher who regards the piece as having "high artistic power" remarks at the same time, "In the piece the author indulges only in personal emotions, so it has little significance for society. The tone of the entire piece is too subdued and depressing." Another teacher, who is aware of the cultural bias swaying his evaluation but ranks it the last nevertheless, ruminates, "If I were to apply the same standard to this piece as I do to my Chinese students, I would have to place it the last. It is not enough to just say 'Life would have gotten better.' For a Chinese youth, one should dig deep to find the social causes for such a tragedy. But maybe such a standard is unreasonable for an American student."

But five teachers, out of the twenty-three, think otherwise. Three of them think the piece ends with a positive note, and two others suggest that the piece has certain depth, for it exposes indirectly some social problems.

To conclude, the result of the survey of "To a Friend" is far different from the overall positive responses I heard from the four principal teachers, but it does not come as a total surprise. Although none of the four teachers questioned its credence and moral ramification, both Jack and Mr. Zhang pointed out that the relationship between the author and her friend was not fully developed, and Jack warned that American teachers might consider the piece too sentimental. The cultural divide is most evident in regard to the "raw" emotion in the piece. Most Chinese teachers respond to the piece as Mr. Wang and Mr. Zhang did: instead of calling it "phony" or "sentimental," they are deeply moved. That is in sharp contrast to the strong rejection by most American respondents. Either the Chinese readers are a credulous and maudlin lot, easily overpowered by emotion, or they simply have a different criteria for what is "phony," and, for that matter, what is good writing. One American respondent explains, "Strength of feeling alone does not establish an appropriate and sustainable relationship between the writer and reader." He certainly cannot speak for how the Chinese reader relates to the writer, for whom emotion, instead of short-circuiting the relationship, jump-starts it.

On the other hand, a good number of Chinese respondents, whose major objection to the piece is the absence of an uplifting and socially significant message, would have a hard time finding an ally among their American colleagues who would share their concern with the social significance of student writing.

CHAPTER 4

One Researcher's Perspective

A fine professor of mine once told me that, in doing research, a disciplined researcher should always concentrate on "hows," because facts, and facts alone, provide the sure route to truth. So far, I have followed his advice, documenting as faithfully as possible the data gathered from the field, staying on the course of fact-finding and fact-telling. In this final chapter, however, I will take advantage of my outsider-insider double identity and adopt a comparative approach to discuss the differences and similarities of the two cultures' criteria for "good writing," thus venturing into the murky water of "whys." The discussion will draw on the information gathered in the study, that is, the interviews with the four principal teachers and the survey. It will also draw on the research and scholarly works on literary theory in both countries. When one goes beyond the mere recording of facts to sort out the causal, logical, and historical connections among the facts, there is always the risk of engaging in speculation. I take the plunge anyway.

So, what is good writing? It is tempting, after glancing at the results of the survey according to which each piece received at least three different rankings from the participant of either country, to conclude that "good writing" is just a matter of personal taste. Well it is, and it is not. It is a splice of multiple linguistic and nonlinguistic, cultural and historical strands; of what is written in a piece and the manner in which the piece is written; of ideology and aesthetic; of society and individuals. As we see in the survey, American teachers might not give the same grade to a paper, but few would criticize a paper for its lack of "significant social consequences," as many Chinese teachers did. Chinese teachers, likewise, might disagree among themselves as to which was the best paper, but few would select one because of its "ambivalent and provocative ending." What most Chinese teachers saw as an expression of "honest, strong and sincere emotions," was seen by most American teachers as "uncontrollable, almost peevish." And the American teachers' insatiable appetite for realistic details could be matched only by their Chinese counterparts' rapture over poetic images. Teacher evaluators, after all, are not beyond the reach of cultural impacts. Even the rebels in a society invariably bear the stamps of the society they claim to fight. Radical students in the sixties in America, for example, may have held Mao's red book, but would they have settled in poverty-stricken areas when Mao instructed them to do so and as legions of Chinese Red Guards did without a second thought? Would Chinese Red Guards, on the other hand, have swarmed to Woodstock if it had been held in China in the sixties? Would they have considered free love and rock-n-roll as declarations of rebellion? I seriously doubt that the answer would be in the affirmative in either case. We would like to think of ourselves as free agents independent of institutional constrains, yet, setting aside material restraints, freedom goes only as far as our imagination carries us. Cross-cultural studies, with the mission of looking closely at how other cultures deal with the same challenges of life, provide a felicitous means to stretch our imagination. In this chapter I will focus on areas in the study where the forces of the language and society manifested themselves prominently in shaping the conception of "good writing" in America and China.

WRITING, A VEHICLE OF *TAO*

In the study, teachers' evaluations of the student paper often started from the construction of the writer's intention. Whether the construction was performed consciously or subconsciously, it directly affected the outcome of the evaluation. As Flower observes, despite the postmodern doubts of the validity of the "authorial intention," good writing teachers are still expected to "infer the purpose(s) behind a student's text"(528). Teachers do so, in teaching, to help students realize unfulfilled intentions, and, in evaluation, to decide how successful the writing actually realizes the writer's intention. Yet the purpose of a text, as Flower points out, is located both in the text itself and the in the linguistic and social context of the text. The evaluation goes awry when the teacher evaluator does not share the same social and linguistic context with the student writer. Unless particular caution is taken, the teacher evaluator, who holds more power in the reader-writer-text triangle, is prone to impose her own frame of reference on the text and the writer, expecting the writer to fulfill unintended purposes.

The study provides ample evidence in this regard. "Me, Before and After the Exam," for example, was read by the American teachers involved as one on "decision-making" or "the love of nature," while it was obvious to the Chinese teachers that "conquering self" was the message that the writer intended. Given the linguistic context within which they operate, it is not hard to understand why the American teachers misread the writer's intention, which was, to the Chinese teachers, stated explicitly in the episode of "Mother's advice," when the writer's mother quoted from Indian leader Nehru's words: "in everyday life, a hero is someone who can conquer himself." "To conquer self," however, is a phrase I manufactured in translation. I tried other more idiomatic phrases like "take control of oneself," "make up one's own mind," "make peace with oneself," et cetera, but still settled for the non-English phrase, because only "to conquer self," a literal translation of the Chinese phrase, conveys the sense of struggle and triumph the original Chinese, possibly also Hindu, connotes. *Decision-making,* on the other hand, is a term in Chinese referring to an activity limited to people who hold power, especially those who hold high ranks in the government. It is thus absolutely out of place when applied to a child facing a moral dilemma. Mr. Wang and Mr. Zhang, or any other Chinese teachers, would not be able to infer such purpose from the piece even if they stretched their imagination.

"River in My Hometown" is, by comparison, a fortunate case, because, as principal teacher Jane commented, "our ancestors had it tough" is a universal theme. Maybe it is, although in America it is part of the frontier mythology, and in China it has strong political implications. Comparing the tough life in the past (i.e., before the year of 1949) with the happy life at the present has been used as a powerful means of political education in China since 1949, the year when the Communists took over the country. It serves the purpose of telling the people that "When drinking water, don't forget who dug the well; When living a good life, don't forget the Party." So the deeper meaning of the piece, as pointed out by Mr. Zhang, was to show the superiority of the socialist system brought about by the Communist Party. But if that motif had ever occurred to Jane, the piece would have been seen as a piece of propaganda, which, thanks to decades of the Cold War, is a devil term in American language and psyche.

Some of the problems the Chinese teachers had with "Beat Them 'til They're Black and Blue" can be attributed to the same misconstrual of the purpose of the piece. It is no accident that none of the Chinese readers thought of the piece as being about the inexplicability of human relationships and life itself, as Jack and other American teachers did. (It is only fair to point out, though, that a good number of American readers did not get it either, but for different reasons, I believe, from what it presented here for the Chinese teachers' reading.) A piece that intends to present life as an inexplicable mystery would be deemed by Chinese readers, especially ones trained in orthodox Marxism, as one that advocates an agnostic view of reality. Agnosticism is defined in the *Ci Hai* (Ocean of Words), one of the most comprehensive and authoritative Chinese encyclopedias, as:

> A philosophy that advocates the inaccessibility of the essence of matter and truth other than their impressions and outward manifestations. . . . It opens the the the door to religions. Some schools in modern bourgeois philosophy (such as Mach and pragmatism) advocate it to preempt the oppressed classes from knowing the truth.

So to believe that life is inexplicable is to fall for bourgeois ideology and is directly opposed to Marxist dialectical materialism. Therefore it was, to the Chinese teachers, an inappropriate and impossible theme for a student paper. Although praised by some Chinese teachers for creating the effect of "suspense" and "contrast," the piece was not seen as a successful realization of the writer's intention. Consequently, despite most Chinese teachers' enthusiasm for the piece in general, it was judged as being vague and incomplete, and was ranked in second place by most Chinese participants of the survey, who read it not as an illustration or a philosophy on life and human relationships, but simply an half-aborted portrayal of an enigmatic character.

What follows the construction of the writer's purposes is the teacher's judgment of the soundness of the theme. The Chinese teachers usually started their comments with a summary statement of their understanding of the subject matter, such as, "It portrays an admirable character," or "It describes the psychological process of. . . ." Then they proceeded to evaluate the social significance of the piece, a step few American teachers took. The assessment of a piece's social impact accounted for much of the criticism from the Chinese teachers of "To a Friend," and some of "Beat Them 'til They're Black and Blue." A Chinese respondent, much fascinated by the mystery of "Grandpa," nevertheless remarked, ". . . it portrays an unfathomable strange old man, which does not have the same significance as 'There is an Old Lady.'" The criticism of "To a Friend" is more concerted, despite the fact many Chinese teachers claimed that they were deeply moved by the piece. As one teacher explained, "If I am to apply the same standard to this piece as I do to my Chinese students, I have to place it the last. It is not enough to just say 'Life would have gotten better.' For a Chinese youth, one should dig deep to find the social causes for such a tragedy." Another commented, ". . . the author indulges only in personal emotions, so it has little significance for the society." The pieces written by the Chinese students were scrutinized just as rigorously. The theme of "Me, Before and After the Exam" was praised by most Chinese teachers, but the piece was railed at by some as portraying "a decision to indulge a personal hobby," or by others as showing "insensitivity to others' feelings." Chinese teachers are obliged by the Chinese tradition and the current political system to be the gatekeepers of social morality and ethics, a role not expected of American teachers.

The idea that writing is a vehicle and not an object of pursuit in and of itself was probably first proposed by China's consummate teacher, Confucius, and reinforced by consecutive Chinese rulers, the last being the late chairman of the Chinese Communist Party, Mao Tze-tong. The role of Confucianism in Chinese society is characterized by de Bary et al. in *Sources of Chinese Tradition* in this way: "it has become an inseparable part of the society and thought of the nation as a whole, of what it means to be a Chinese, as the Confucian Classics are not the canon of a particular sect but the literary heritage of a whole people" (15). Confucius's absolute authority first came under attack during the May Fourth Movement in 1919, the precursor of the Communist movement in China. One of the slogans in that movement was "Down with the Confucius Shop!" After the Communists took over China in 1949, Confucius's classics, including *Lun Yu* (commonly known in English as the *Analects of Confucius*), were taken off the school curriculum (except in Taiwan, where the Nationalist Party has been ruling). The attack on Confucianism and Confucius reached its peak during the Cultural Revolution. In line with the highly belligerent rhetoric of the time, Confucius was called, among other things, "Supreme master of feudal ideology," "crafty hypocrite," and "political swindler." When I went back for the research of this project in 1991, I was truly surprised to find that after the Cultural Revolution Confucianism was still alive and well and that Confucius was still revered by the teachers I met. Confucianism has such strong and deep roots in Chinese consciousness that more than forty years of education of Communism and political movements failed to eradicate its influence.

Born in a time, he called, when "the rites decayed and music ruined," Confucius suffered from the outcome of the disintegration of the powerful Chou dynasty into a number of small states constantly at war with each other, and from the decline of his own family from nobility to poverty and insignificance. He was convinced from early on that the restoration of the past glory lay in the restoration of the rule of past moral values. Social stability and prosperity, he told those few who were willing to listen, was based on the fulfillment of the moral contract between the ruler and the ruled. As one of his famous sayings goes, "If you govern the people by virtue, you may be compared to the Pole-star, which keeps its place, while all the other stars revolve round it." The exact content of virtue is discussed at length in *Lun Yu*, a collection of his sayings by his disciples shortly after his death in 497 B.C. What is more relevant here is that Confucius believed such virtue was acquired through learning. Unlike Plato, who bestows philosophers the highest place in social hierarchy and teachers the eighth place (in the same slot with demagogues), Confucius ranked people according to their attitude towards learning: "Those who are born with knowledge are the highest. Next come those who attain knowledge through study. Next again come those who turn to study after having been vexed by difficulties. The common people, insofar as they make no effort to study even after having been vexed by difficulties, are the lowest" (16.9). Confucius did not view himself as one born with knowledge, but as the less privileged second kind, those who "attain knowledge through study." "I was not born with knowledge," he told his disciples, "but, being fond of antiquity, I am quick to seek it" (7.20). Confucius was credited with opening the first public school in China, and he was a life-long teacher, whose mission was "to transmit, not to create." He viewed learning as a prerequisite for innovation. "There are," he warned, "presumably men who innovate without possessing knowledge, but that is not a fault I have" (7.28). Writing, in consonance with his proposed goal of learning, was "the vehicle of *Tao*." *Tao* here covers the sum total of truths about the universe and man, which should govern the mind and the acts of both individuals and the state.

If confronted, it is unlikely that Confucius would be persuaded by the American educational philosophy, which privileges creativity over the acquisition of knowledge, nor would he succumb to the accusation that his brand of education is nothing but "regurgitation" that "perpetuates the status quo," since there is no indication that Confucius ever shared the optimism Americans have in the future and spontaneous human creativity. If in his life the present was worse than the past, why should Confucius believe that the future would be better than the present and that the status quo should be interrupted or destroyed for a dubious future? He would also be hard pushed to accept that a transmissive education would stunt the learner's capacity for innovation, for, if anything, he would probably argue that human ingenuity would not blossom without the fertilization of knowledge. Confucianism was produced by an uncertain and chaotic time, just as American pragmatism, spearheaded by James and further envisioned by educators like Dewey, was begotten by the onset of industrialization at the turn of the century, promising a bountiful future engined and engineered by human initiatives and ingenuity.

Communism in China failed to diminish Confucius's influence, perhaps because Communism has more in common with Confucianism than either was willing to admit. In his "Talks at the Yanan Forum on Literature and Art," hailed as laying down the fundamental guidelines for proletarian creative arts, Mao played the same transmissive role as Confucius did, stating, "Proletarian literature and art are part of the whole proletarian revolutionary cause; they are, as Lenin said, cogs and wheels in the whole revolutionary machine" (82). In Mao's talk, Lenin, instead of the rituals and rites of the Chou dynasty, sets the sacred precedent, and literature is "cogs and wheels" instead of a "vehicle." In either case, whether writing is used to maintain a moral order or to facilitate social changes, it is a means, not an end, the ultimate end lying invariably outside the writing itself and the interest of the writer as an individual. And its success is measured by its effectiveness in meeting those ends. Other criteria are secondary. Mao was very direct about this; in the same talk, he elucidates, "In literary and art criticism there are two criteria, the political and the artistic. . . .each class in every class society has its own political and artistic criteria. But all classes in all class societies invariably put the political criterion first and the artistic criterion second" (84–90). Terry Eagleton and other Marxist critics will not argue with that, but those who believe that "literature is by definition a form of discourse that has no designs on the world" (Tompkins, 125) probably will protest what they view as a shortchanging of the arts for some earthly goal and reducing it to a political means. The fact that most American teachers in the study took the stance of a disinterested evaluator seems to suggest that the attitude towards literature as criticized by Eagleton and Tompkins still dominates. Rather than asking what good a piece is for society, the American teachers seemed more interested in the writer. As one teacher, after reading "There was an Old Lady," asked the author, "What did you learn about yourself?" Self is both the subject and object of the quest, it seems.

Whether literature, and by extension student writing, is a "vehicle" or a goal in itself is a debate that will continue as long as there are believers in either theory. Yet it will be interesting to see whether the capitalist market economy, now making rapid inroads in China, will accomplish what Communism failed in the past century: to shake Confucianism, which has held Chinese minds for more than two thousand years, and turn the "vehicle of *Tao*" to bestsellers. It will be equally interesting to see whether the recent call for the "creation of a moral society" by some educators in the United States (Warehime, xxxiv) will be accepted in American writing classes, where such calls have traditionally been met with aversion.

SPECIFICS, SPECIFICS, SPECIFICS . . .

If the American teachers, as the study suggests, were cautious not to impose their judgment on the moral propriety of student writing, they were certainly less restrained in making judgment concerning the propriety of the narrative style in student writing. The credibility of a piece was a prominent and recurring theme in principal teacher Jane's discussion of student papers and was one of the most frequently evoked criteria in the survey. It is not that the Chinese teachers do not concern themselves with the credibility of student writing, because as Mr. Wang told us, honesty is viewed as a moral issue. Yet the judgment of the credibility of a piece by the Chinese teachers is based on the plausibility of the story and the characters rather than the propriety of its narrative style. A Chinese teacher, one of the few who had doubts about the truthfulness of "Exam," remarked in his commentary on the piece, "If the teacher did not know there was a conflict in schedule between two exams, the student should have reported it to the teachers, especially after the teacher had spent several lunch breaks to tutor her, yet the student did not even give her any hint." He thus concluded: ". . . the events narrated and emotions expressed in the piece are not necessarily true." The question of credibility, for most American readers, however, is a question of the narrative style.

"Me, before and after the Exam" again is a case at hand. Its credence was called into serious question for what was described by one American teacher as the use of a "heavy-handed" narrative style. The teacher described his reaction to the piece as: ". . . I end up not 'believing' the story emotionally, however much I may approve intellectually of its outcome." Notice the quotation marks he placed around the word "believing." I would venture to suggest that his emotional disbelief is an intuitive reaction to a piece that just did not have the right flavor, despite its flawless substance. The critical ingredient lacking in the piece is "to show and not to tell." Such is what another American teacher advised the writer: "show, don't tell—the reader wants to be actively involved rather than spoon-fed." The lack of the showing of specifics also accounted for the low ranking of "To a Friend." One typical comment reads, "No clear picture, doesn't show, could have been written by anyone." And another reader stated directly, "I suspect she never had the experience."

It is evident from the study that to "use definite, specific, concrete language" is one maxim that is followed with almost religious exactitude by most American teachers. Hirsch found the same result after he reviewed five popular handbooks used in American writing classes: Strunk, Gowers, McCrimmon, Crews, and Lucas (Ohmann, 379).[1]

It is hard to pinpoint where this American precept of good writing came from, but one can see this precept at work when one reads realistic novels that boomed around the turn of the century and still enjoy wide popularity in this postmodern era in America. One common feature of such novels is that they are all filled with circumstantial, matter-of-fact, and seemingly unselective details. Realism, as defined by Nochlin, aims to "give a truthful, objective and impartial representation of the real world, based on meticulous observation of contemporary life" (13).

Plato is believed to be the first one who espoused the mimetic theory of art, but he also despised art, for he holds that truth lies beyond appearance; the best painting of a bed, therefore, is just an "imitation of an imitation" and no good to sleep on either (Sontag 3). Although Aristotle defended the usefulness of art—he believed that art has the function to arouse and purge dangerous emotions—he never challenged Plato's view of art as mimesis. The present study also supports Sontag's observation that "all Western consciousness of and reflection upon art have remained within the confines staked out by the Greek theory of art as mimesis or representation," and that "even in modern times, when most artists and critics have discarded the theory of art as representation of an outer reality in favor of the theory of art as subjective expression, the main feature of the mimetic theory persists" (4). Which means that although the walls of the Guggenheim Museum in Soho, New York, are lined with abstract paintings and sculptures that intentionally distort or exaggerate natural forms and colors, such art has only a small following. The limited success of modern art in revolutionizing the means of expression is seen in the teachers' criteria for "good writing." American teachers did encourage students to explore their inner, subjective world, but they still expected students to represent their interior worlds as mimetically, as when they represent the exterior world, that is, by using multitudinous definite, specific, concrete details. The narrators of "Exam" and "To a Friend" violated the basic maxim of writing, which in turn undermined their credibility as reliable narrators.

Ohmann, a rare exception among the composition specialists in America, questioned the ideological implications of this maxim of good writing. In his article "Use Definite, Specific, Concrete Language" he contends that such a criterion conveys an ideological bias for "ahistoricism" (focusing on a truncated present moment), "empiricism" (favoring sensory information from the surface of things), "fragmentation" (seeing an object in isolation, disconnected from the rest of the world), "solopisism" (privileging the writer's own perception), and "denial of conflict" (picturing a world in which all readers read the same meaning into the details presented). Furthermore, Ohmann argues, such stylistic preference "pushes the student writer always toward the language that most neatly reproduces the immediate experience and away from the language that might be used to understand it, transform it, and relate it to everything else" (387–388). Ohmann is a well-respected scholar in America and his article was published in 1979 and later anthologized in the well-circulated *Writing Teacher's Sourcebook*. It is not surprising, though, that when this study was conducted, little had changed. A tradition, once established, acquires a life of its own.

Some teachers in the study argued that "to show and not to tell" was a democratic sharing of power between writers and readers. Writers show their experience and readers draw their own independent conclusions. It is a transgressing of readers' rights to tell them what the piece is about. Americans' resentment towards telling is manifest in teenagers, who impatiently wave their patents away with "Don't tell me what to do!"

Chinese children, on the other hand, are used to being told by parents, teachers, and any other senior people. Although they don't always listen, showing deference to the authority, to the more experienced and knowledgeable, is expected. Chinese readers, likewise, do not mind being told either. Actually if writing is by nature didactic, as Confucius says, it is the writer's responsibility to tell.

The preference for multitudinous specifics is, in addition, at odds with a Chinese literary tradition that prefers a densely selective and suggestive narrative style. The example related by Mr. Zhang of Shuisheng's wife in the prose "Lotus-flower Lake" by the highly acclaimed Chinese writer Sun Li is a good illustration of the style. One specific detail, "for a second, the woman's fingers' quivered," is all the information the writer provides, leaving the reader to imagine the emotional turmoil Shuisheng's wife experienced when she heard that her husband was leaving for the battlefield. American readers probably would find that description, though definite and specific, too sparse to be engaging, but for Chinese readers, a few well-chosen details can make more intense and engaging writing than one filled with volumes of details, which most Chinese readers find ponderous and boring. Even *Dream of the Red Chamber*, full of delicious and minute details of life inside the great mansion, which many believe is the greatest realistic novel Chinese literature ever produced, is punctuated by the narrator's interjection warning the reader of the false sense of reality created by life-like details. The couplet in the "Land of Illusion," where the heavenly truth is confided, reads "When the unreal is taken for the real, then the real becomes unreal; Where nonexistence is taken for existence, then existence becomes nonexistence." It bears an eerie resemblance to Plato's criticism of art as an imitation of "mere appearances." The narrator, I dare to suggest, by assuming a realistic style, is actually accentuating the deceptiveness of the seemingly real. I am not suggesting, nevertheless, that the Chinese preference for high selectivity of details proceeded from the Buddhist outlook on life, anymore than I believe that "to show and not to tell" sprang wholly from democratic principles. I would rather attribute the Chinese preference for the condensed style to the peculiar place of poetry in Chinese literary history. Until the last century poetry had been revered in China as the only form of literary creation worthy of aspiration. As the translator of *Dream of the Red Chamber* tells us in the preface to its English version, the book was written at a time when "the novel was regarded, as it had always been, an outcast of literature and was written or compiled largely by unknown hacks. If a rare self-respecting literocrat should, for one reason or another, undertake to write an original novel, he did so largely for his own amusement, without any idea of publication. He would not even sign his name to his work." Tsao, the author, died in 1764 with the novel unfinished. In the novel, though, the male and female protagonists are all accomplished poets, thus conveniently giving Tsao sufficient opportunities to demonstrate his talent as a accomplished poet and, perhaps, to redeem his indulgence in the trivial art of "small talk." Poetry is a highly condensed form of writing, especially with Chinese poetry, the normal length of which is usually four or eight lines, each of five or seven monosyllabic characters. There were longer narrative poems, but never did China have such epic poems as the *Odyssey* and the *Iliad*.

China has a long tradition of abstract and realistic art (neither in the Western sense, though). Chinese Peking Opera uses exaggerated colors and patterns in the facial make-up. The stage in a Peking Opera is bare, with a few symbolic props. A desk, for example, can be a mountain, a city wall, a castle, or just a desk. Sometimes, with a talented director, it can be a number of things in the same show. Traditional Chinese ink painting leaves large blank spaces for viewers to fill up with their imagination. Li Tungyang, a poet of the Ming Dynasty, draws an analogy between an ink painting of bamboos and writing: ". . . complexity is hard, yet simplicity is harder. You see only a dark bamboo shaking with a few thin leaves, but you can feel the raging storm and withering cold" (Zhou, 355).

Realism started with the emergence of novels and gained greater popularity after the May Fourth Movement, when foreign works of literature, mostly from Europe and Russia, were translated in large numbers. Yet when realism was transplanted to China, it was adapted to Chinese readers' palates. China has never produced a Dickens or Tolstoy. Mao characterized revolutionary realism as "a literature that is from life but more typical than ordinary life." (234). Typicality is still preferred to mimesis, realism or not.

To the American teachers, a credible narrator, the study suggests, is one that possesses certain type of temperament. He should be restrained, detached, and controlled, rather than sentimental, dramatic, and emotionally involved. I use the pronoun "he" intentionally, because those preferred qualities add up to a cool guy, and the rejected qualities are the ones usually associated with femininity. Yet it is not just an issue of gender; it is one of culture as well. The Chinese teachers in the survey, male or female, were all deeply moved by "To a Friend." Although some of them questioned the thematic significance of the piece, no one questioned its honesty and credibility. The American readers, in contrast, were deeply skeptical of or averse to what they described as a "gush." One of them expressed his ambivalence and distrust as ". . . while I *want* to feel strongly about what happened, and I think I *ought* to feel strongly about what happened, I just don't" (the emphasis is in original). Another piece that did not do well in the survey was "Me, Before and After the Exam," which was also called "phony," "pathetic," and "sentimental" by a good number of American readers, one of whom even suggested that the piece was probably modeled after "some second-rate eighteenth- or nineteenth-century prose."

Chinese writing often gives American readers the impression of being overdramatic and overtly sentimental. An American teacher who taught writing in China for a year had this to say about what he read in China: "Chinese prose . . . is full of old-fashioned Victorian sugaring— long verbal signs, clutched body parts, and grand exhalations of feeling. The Chinese are, after all, like the Italians, an operatic culture" (Holm, 60). What is viewed by Westerners as sentimentality is also related to the long Chinese love affair with poetry. The nature of poetry is crystallized in the aphorism "Poetry is the words of the heart *[shi1 yan2 zhi4]*," which are said to be the words of the legendary Sage-Emperor Shun[2] (Liu, 69). The division of heart and mind is a Western phenomenon. Heart, according to Chinese tradition, is the organ responsible for both intelligence and sentiments. This ancient notion has been preserved in Chinese characters like think *[xiang3]*, anger *[nu4]*, feel *[gan3]*, all having the same radical component: heart *[xin1]*. In his seminal work, *History of Chinese Philosophy*, Feng You-lan proposes that "the Confucianist and Taoist traditions in Chinese history are in some degree equivalent to the classical and romantic traditions in the West" (232). There is some truth to his analogy. An ideal man of Confucianism transcends the material world, never perturbed by the loss and gain of fame and fortune, yet a sage is not devoid of emotions. The difference between an ordinary man and a sage, says Wang Pi, a Confucius scholar, is that a sage "has emotions but is not ensnared by them" (Feng, 238). Liu Xie, who authored the first comprehensive review of Chinese critical theories, summarizes the principles of literature in the following way:

> The basic way of literature consists of three principles: the first is called the "formal pattern," which refers to the five colors; the second is called the "auditory pattern," which refers to the five notes; the third is called the "emotional pattern," which refers to the five temperaments. The five colors, when interwoven, form embroidered patterns; the five notes, when arranged, form music such as the Shao and the Xia;[3] the five temperaments, when expressed, form literary compositions: this is the inevitable working of divine principles. (Liu, 102)

What is missing from the three principles, as a Westerner will quickly discern, is logic and reasoning. Five temperaments, instead of one particular type of temperament, are believed by the Chinese to make fine literature. In the West, one apologizes for weeping in public, but in China it is not unmanly, but noble in certain circumstances, to shed tears for the tragic and express anger for the unjust. Even after the introduction of realism in the fifties through the influx of foreign literature, romanticism is never rejected or replaced. Mao Tze-tung states that the right style of revolutionary literature should be "a combination of revolutionary romanticism and revolutionary realism."

Modernism, characterized by Suzanne Clark as a representation of life that "emphasized erotic desire, not love; anarchic rupture and innovation rather than the conventional appeals of sentimental language" (1), is a direct revolt against Romanticism. T.S Eliot's scorn for Romantic poetry was typical of his time, "Poetry had fallen foul of the Romantics, become a mawkish, womanly affair full of gush and fine feeling" (Eagleton, 41). The rejection of Romanticism and the rise of Modernism in the West was synchronous with the growing popularity of Freud's theory on human psychology, which Jung believed was responsible for the ultimate disillusionment of human nature. Jung claims: "The end-product of the Freudian method of explanation is a detailed elaboration of man's shadow-side such as had never been carried out before. It is the most effective antidote imaginable to all idealistic illusions about the nature of man . . ." (40). According to Freud, the human psyche is the victim of one's unfulfilled libidinous desires and is inflicted forever with fear, neuroses, Oedipus complexes, et cetera. All those traditional sentiments for romantic love, for selfless sacrifice, for common good and social justice are thus nothing but one's phony fronts to conform to a repressive outer world. For those who believe that there is a Hyde under every Jekyll, writing that promotes the sunny side of human nature must appear hopelessly magnanimous or downright pretentious. Such antiromanticism, for better or for worse, has not been shared by Chinese readers, who are unaffected by Freudianism. A detached narrator is viewed by Chinese readers not as cool but, more likely, as cold and heartless; a piece of writing that ends with a noncommittal conclusion would strike them as incomplete; a narrator who scoffs at positive human sentiments and good human nature is likely to be perceived as a bitter cynic rather than a sophisticated realist. It is not certain, though, that only Chinese readers are prone to what Eliot calls "a mawkish, womanly affair full of gush and fine feeling." The fact that the so-called sentimental novel *Uncle Tom's Cabin* stirred America into a prolonged war against slavery, and that Harlequin romances are sold in millions in American supermarkets, suggests that the squeamishness about sentimentalism is, rather than a sweeping cultural phenomenon, but a special trait of some literary elitists.

NATURAL LANGUAGE AND ORGANIC STRUCTURE

Finally there is the most elusive criterion of being "natural," an epithet frequently evoked in the survey and in interviews of teachers from both countries. If being "natural" means unrefined or uncrafted, "To a Friend," a direct outpouring of the writer's sentiments without much embellishment, should be judged as a natural piece, yet it is ranked last in the survey by teachers of both countries and was scathed as "raw, uncrafted, unedited" and "unnatural" by some American readers. Such evaluation makes one wonder what "natural" really means, for obviously it does not mean that students can simply write in their "natural voices"; they have to conform to certain criteria in order to be natural.

Natural writing presumably creates a casual feel by using informal languages and "organic" structures. Yet just as the casual look in fashion is a look that strikes a delicate balance between elegance and informality, natural writing has to strike the right notes. As Jack points out, the appropriate language is between four and five on a continuum from one to ten, ten being the most formal and rigid. It is a language that sounds like talking, but is actually more polished and perfected than everyday speech. To achieve such a delicate balance between the formal and the colloquial does not come naturally. It is an acquired skill.

The belief that there is an organic structure, a structure that grows out the content, like the colors of the flowers born out of nature without the contamination of human hands, echoes the Romantic view of writing as a "spontaneous overflow of powerful feelings," or the dream of Realism "to escape from the bonds of convention into a magic world of pure verisimilitude" (Nochlin, 14).

Naturalness has always been regarded among Chinese artists as the highest achievement of art. Is natural art an oxymoron? No, if one believes that the really smart always appear dumb, and that the best art bears no traces of human hands, as the Chinese are told. Novice writers, therefore, in order to attain natural art, have to start from the unnatural, that is, learning "patterns" and "embellishment," the original meanings of the Chinese character for literature, *wen*. It is commonly believed that Confucius once said, "If writing does not have *wen*, it will not travel afar." Whether Confucius actually said that or not is hard to prove, but since the idea of *wen* is attributed to the Sage, the notion that patterns and embellishment are essential for good writing is well accepted by Chinese writers. Even Mao Tze-tung, who rejected Confucianism as too conservative and insisted that in judging literature the political criteria should come first, sounded like Confucius when he stated, "Works of art which lack artistic quality have no force, however progressive they are politically" (90). The attention to the craft of writing could go to extremes, as happened in the Song Dynasty (420–479 A.D.), when poets were so preoccupied with the perfection of forms that works of literature became mere ornaments, empty of substance. Most Chinese scholars dismiss the ornamental "Song style," but few go so far as to think that writing is "pure verisimilitude" of reality, and that the form of a piece of writing takes care of itself if the writer takes care of its substance.

The difference between oral and written language is very distinct in Chinese too. Owing to the abundance of homophones in Chinese language, oral language is, by necessity, composed mostly of polysyllabic words, while the written language, since the homophones are distinguishable as characters, uses monosyllables, which also contributes to the highly condensed style of writing. A piece written in classic Chinese, as a result, can be totally unintelligible even to an educated ear when read aloud, not to speak of those who have no education. The gap between written and spoken language was reduced after the May Fourth Movement in 1919,[4] yet the difference is still large. The written language is now a mixture of the classic with the vernacular, yet still unmistakably distinct from the way one talks. The heavy use of four-syllable proverbs, of formal dictions, and the frequent employment of images and symbols, are telling marks of the written language. The goal of the vernacularization of Chinese written language, in addition, was to make literacy more accessible to the uneducated, rather than to uncover the authentic personal "voice" or to duplicate reality.

Nochlin addresses a common issue of literary creation that is not confined to realistic writing when she comments, "Realism was no more a mere mirror of reality than any other style and its relation *qua* style to phenomenal data—the *donnee*—is as complex and difficult as that of Romanticism, the Baroque, or Mannerism" (14). Nochlin knows, as do great writers who spend hours sweating over the pages to perfect their product, that the seeming "total spontaneity" or "a magic world of pure verisimilitude" are illusions created by masterful artists. In other words, it is cultivated nature.

There are other differences in the criteria of good writing between the two countries, which were well explained by the principal teachers, such as American teachers' emphasis on flawless logic and an opening that leads the reader immediately to the action, and Chinese teachers' peculiar propensity for the mingling of *qing* (human emotions) with *jing* (natural scenes) and their preference for a "dragon's eye" at the end to bring the piece to a definitive closure. Most important is their different perceptions of the role of teachers, whether as transmitters of tradition and knowledge or as facilitators of self-expression. Their divergence on this fundamental issue, as I expounded before, lies at the heart of all other differences.

Ever since linguist Robert Kaplan initiated the study of cross-cultural rhetorics (1966), much research has been done on students' writing from different cultural backgrounds. The recent publication of *Writing Across Languages and Cultures*, edited by Alan Purves, indicates the growing interest in cross cultural studies in the field of composition studies. While it is important to acknowledge that "good writing" is culturally situated, we should also be aware of the pitfall of attributing all problems in the writing of students from other backgrounds to cultural differences to avoid the same mistake made by linguists when contrastive analysis (CA) was first introduced in the study of second-language acquisition. CA studies have proved useful not only for pedagogical purposes but for our understanding of the operations of languages in general, yet CA cannot explain all the problems in second-language acquisition. Dulay and Burt's L2 = L1 theory holds that some of the goofs of L2 learners are similar to those made by children learning that same language as their first language (55). So problems in second-language acquisition could be cultural as well as cognitive. There is plenty of evidence in this study that the two cultures, despite their significant differences, also share many similarities in their criteria for "good writing." Caution notwithstanding, Robert Lado's claim in 1957 that "the individuals tend to transfer the forms and meanings, and the distribution of forms and meanings of their native language and culture to the foreign language and culture" is a real and central phenomenon in the acquisition of the second language. So is it in the teacher's reading of student papers. To make judicious judgment about the sources of students problems, linguists, as well as writing teachers, should acquaint themselves with students' native cultures and languages.

All said, teachers' criteria for "good writing" is a cultivated sensitivity, an acquired taste. Of all the formative factors, one's experience with literature and literary theories is probably the most influential. American teachers' debt to Realism and Modernism is as evident as Chinese teachers' debt to Chinese Romantic poetry and Confucius's classics, as well as to Marxist theories of literature. To write to different standards, according to Fan Shen, is to do more than switch linguistic codes: it is a process of acculturation. He learned from his experience as a Chinese graduate student in an American university that when his American writing professors told him to "be yourself," what they really meant was not to be his Chinese self, but that he "had to create an English self and be that self," that he had to shed his "timid, humble, modest Chinese *I*" and take on the facade of "confident, assertive and aggressive English *I.*" I hope this study on "good writing" in cross-cultural context serves to stretch the imagination of educators in both countries to understand the cultural bias in the standards many of them so rigorously maintain, without having to go through the troublesome experience of Fan Shen.

At the end of his article, Fan Shen relates an anecdote of an American businessman who, ignorant of the Chinese dislike for cheese, gave his Chinese hostess cheddar cheeses as gifts. I hope American readers can now imagine how cheddar cheese would taste to the Chinese after they have tasted the Chinese students' writing and Chinese teachers' comments. You don't have to like "birds nests," an expensive and exquisite Chinese dish, just as most Chinese probably will never learn to like cheddar cheese, but we should learn what Charles Cooper remarks in the preface of *Writing Across Languages and Cultures*: "What may be valued in one culture may be disregarded or even stigmatized in another." Beauty is, indeed, in the eye of the beholder.

NOTES

INTRODUCTION

1. Lu Shun (also spelled Lu Hsun, 1881–1936): a forebear of Chinese modern literature.

2. "Key" schools in China are officially designated on the basis of academic excellence as well as geographic location. Once a school is designated as a key school, it is provided with better teachers and educational facilities, and more importantly, it selects top performers at the entrance exam. The policy is part of the reform program implemented in China after the Cultural Revolution to accelerate "the modernization of science." The theory for such a program is basically economical: to maximize the limited national resources to train the best professionals. It is carried out at all levels, from the elementary to the college.

CHAPTER 1
FOUR TEACHERS AND SIX PIECES (PART 1)

1. All principal teachers' names are changed to protect their confidentiality, which is particularly necessary for political safety of the Chinese teachers. I keep, however, the forms by which I addressed them during the cooperation: the first name with the American teachers and the last with the Chinese teachers, only changing "Teacher" to "Mr." with the Chinese teachers to conform to the American custom.

2. It was one year after the Tiananmen upheaval. The tension between the government and the people, particularly the intellectuals, was still boiling beneath the surface, and it was rumored that all mail abroad was censored.

3. The Chinese transliteration of important concepts and sayings is provided in italics in the spelling of *Pinyin*, the official alphabetic system of Chinese in Mainland China based on what is known as Mandarin in Western countries. Names of well-known persons, such as Confucius, Mao Tze-tung, etc., use the traditional spelling familiar to the Western readers.

Chinese is a tonal language. Where necessary, tones are indicated with numbers (1: high level; 2: rising; 3: fall-rise; 4: falling)

4. The six arts are propriety, music, archery, charioteering, writing, and counting.

5. Du Fu, also translated Tu Fu (712–770): known as one of the best poets of the High Tang Dynasty.

6. Tao Yuanming (365?–427): a recluse poet in the East Jin Dynasty.

7. Chinese ancient unit for dry measures.

8. Li Bai (also translated Li Po, 701–762): along with Du Fu , his contemporary and good friend, are viewed as the two best poets China ever produced, who raised poetry *(shi)* to its highest level of power and expressiveness.

9. Bai Juyi (also translated Po Chu-yi, 772–846): one of the most prolific of the major Tang Poets; first a government official and then a poet in exile because of his outspoken criticism of government policy.

10. The italics indicate that the original Chinese is written with four-character phrases, known as proverbs, with a very rhythmic effect. Here the adverbial consists of four such phrases.

11. The original four-character phrase literarily means: (with) one stumble, one slip.

12. The literary translation of the original four-character phrase is: like grieving, like crying.

13. A line taken from a well-known poem.

CHAPTER 2
FOUR TEACHERS AND SIX PIECES (PART 2)

1. Both *shi* and *ci* mean poetry in English, yet they are different. *Ci* is written to certain singing tunes, which require strict tonal patterns and rhyming schemes. It originated in the Tang Dynasty (618–907) and was fully developed in the Song Dynasty (960–1279). It is generally believed that Chinese poetry reached its pinnacle in Tang and Song and was never surpassed thereafter.

2. An Shi Mutiny (755 A.D.): a mutiny led by General An and General Shi, which ended the Tang Dynasty, and inflicted much hardship on the populace. It is an incident recurred most frequently in, say, Du Fu's poems.

3. The Ming Dynasty spans from 1368 to 1644, and the Qing Dynasty from 1644 to 1911.

4. "Fresh" in Chinese is a homonym of *qing* in Qing Dynasty.

5. Su Tongpo (1037–1101), poet, painter, and social reformer.

6. Zhuangzi (around 369–286 B.C.): a philosopher, he is often mentioned in same ranking with Confucius in Chinese philosophy, and his works are regarded as classics of Taoism.

7. *Possession* by A. S.Byatt, published by Vintage (New York, 1990).

8. *Waterside:* one of the three most popular Chinese classic novels. The other two are *Dream of the Red Chamber* and *The Tale of Three Kingdoms.*

9. *Annals by Zuo* is part of *Thirteen Classics (shi-san jing)*, written in early time of Warring States (475–221 B.C.), known for its rich and authentic historical data and elegant literary style.

10. Wang Guowei (1877–1927): a prominent scholar in modern Chinese drama and poetry. After the bourgeois democratic revolution in 1911, as a staunch loyalist to the last emperor, he drowned himself.

11. *The Book of Odes:* an anthology traditionally believed to have been compiled by Confucius, consists of 305 poems, the earliest extant examples of Chinese poetry. The poems probably dated from around 1000 to 600 B.C.

12. Ling Cong: a major character in *Waterside*, who used to be a *Jiaotao*, equivalent to a sergeant, in the government army, later became one of the 108 rebels in the peasant insurgency.

13. Liu Xie (around 465–532 A.D.): a monk-scholar, who proposed the most systematic literary theories in China.

CHAPTER 4
ONE RESEARCHER'S PERSPECTIVE

1. The second most popular maxim, according to Hirsch, is "avoid padding." Interestingly enough, although Chinese student writing was frequently criticized for straight telling and lacking specifics, it was never criticized as padded.

2. Emperor Shun's life is traditionally dated 2255–2208 B.C.

3. Music of the Shao and the Xia: According to Confucius's classic *On Music,* it is the best music created in ancient China, yet no actual musical script has been found.

4. The May Fourth Movement, 1919, was a nationalist movement triggered by the signing of a humiliating treaty at Paris by the Chinese Government with other superpowers. The movement quickly merged with the then Literary Revolution that started in 1917, which had its chief premise the idea that the archaic classic style of writing should be replaced by a vernacular style called *Baihua* (plain language)—see John DeFrancis, 243.

BIBLIOGRAPHY

Anson, Chris M., ed. *Writing and Responding: Theory, Practice, and Research.* Urbana, IL: National Council of Teachers of English, 1989.

Belenky, Mary F., Blythe M. Clinchy, Nancy R. Goldberger, and Jill M. Tarule. *Women's Ways of Knowing: The Development of Self, Voice, and Mind.* New York: Basic, 1986.

Brannon, Lil, and C. H. Knoblauch. On Students' Rights to Their Own Texts: A Model of Teacher Response. *College Composition and Communication* 33 (1982), 157–166.

———. *Rhetorical Traditions and the Teaching of Writing.* Portsmouth, NH: Boynton/Cook Heinemann, 1984.

Bruner, Jerome. *Actual Minds, Possible Worlds.* Cambridge: Harvard University Press, 1986.

Chen, Dong-yuan. *History of Chinese Education* (in Chinese). Taiwan: Commerce Publishing House, 25 the Chinese National Year.

Clark, Micheal. There Is No Such Thing as Good Writing (So What Are We Looking For?) *Reinventing the Rhetorical Tradition.* Ed. Aviva Freedman and Ian Pringle. Conway, AK: L & S Books, 1980. 129–135.

Clark, Suzanne. *Sentimental Modernism: Women Writers and the Revolution of the Word.* Bloomington: Indiana University Press, 1991.

Coles, William E., and James Vopat. *What Makes Writing Good: A Multiperspective.* Lexington, MA: D. C. Heath, 1985.

Cooper, Charles R. and Lee Odell. *Evaluating Writing.* Urbana, IL: National Council of Teachers of English, 1977.

Corbett, Edward P. "A Method of Analyzing Prose Style with a Demonstration Analysis of Swift's 'A Modest Proposal.'" *The Writing Teacher's Sourcebook.* Ed. Gary Tate and Edward Corbett. New York: Oxford University Press, 1981. 333–352.

Confucius. *The Analects.* Trans. D. C. Lau. New York: Penguin, 1979.

de Bary, William Theodore, et al. 1960. *Sources of Chinese Tradition.* New York: Columbia University Press, 1960.

DeFrancis, John. *The Chinese Language: Fact and Fantasy*. Honolulu: University of Hawaii Press, 1984.

Dennerline, Jerry. 1988. *Qian Mu and the World of Seven Mansions*. New Haven: Yale University Press, 1988.

Dulay, Heidi C., and Marina K. Burt. "Goofing: An Indicator of Children's Second Language Learning Strategies." *Language Transfer in Language Learning*. Ed. Susan Gass and Larry Selinker. London: Newbury House, 1983. 54–68.

Eagleton, Terry. *Literary Theory: an Introduction*. Minneapolis: University of Minnesota Press, 1983.

Earisman, Del. "Holistic Reading in the Composition Class." *College Composition and Communication* 33 (1982), 450–452.

Emig, Janet. "Writing as a Mode of Learning." *The Writing Teacher's Sourcebook*. Ed. Gary Tate and Edward Corbett. New York: Oxford University Press, 1982.

Emig, Janet A., and Robert P. Parker. "Responding to Student Writing: Building a Theory of the Evaluative Process." ERIC ED 136 257.

Feng, You-lan. *A Short History of Chinese Philosophy*. Ed. Derk Bodde. New York: Macmillan, 1953.

Flower, Linda. "The Construction of Purpose in Writing and Reading." *College English* 50 (1988): 528–550.

Freedman, Sarah Warshauer. "Why Do Teachers Give the Grades They Do?" *College Composition and Communication* 30 (1979), 161–164.

Gardner, Howard. *To Open Minds: Chinese Clues to the Dilemma of Contemporary Education*. New York: Basic, 1989.

Geertz, Clifford. "Deep Play: Notes on the Balinese Cockfight." *Ways of Reading*. Ed. David Bartholomae and Anthony Petrosky. Boston: Bedford, 1970, 224–261.

Greenberg, Karen L., Harvey S. Wiener, and Richard A. Donovan, eds. *Writing Assessment: Issues and Strategies*. New York: Longman, 1986.

Griffin, C. W. "Theory of Responding to Student Writing: The State of Art." *College Composition and Communication* 33 (1982): 296–301.

Guba, Egon G., ed. 1990. *The Paradigm Dialog*. Newbury Park, CA: Sage, 1990.

Guba, Egon G., and Y. Lincoln. *Naturalistic Inquiry*. Beverly Hills: Sage.

Heath, Shirley Brice. *Ways with Words: Language, Life, and Work in Communities and Classrooms*. Cambridge: Cambridge University Press, 1983.

Hirsch, E. D. *The Philosophy of Composition.* Chicago: University of Chicago Press, 1977.

Holland, Norman N. *Five Readers Reading,* New Haven: Yale University Press, 1975.

Holm, Bill. *Coming Home Crazy: An Alphabet of China Essays.* Milkweed Education, 1989.

James, William. 1955. *Pragmatism.* 1907. Cleveland: World, 1955.

Jung, Carl G. *Modern Man in Search of a Soul.* New York: Harcourt, Brace, and World, 1933.

Kinneavy, James L. "The Basic Aims of Discourse." *The Writing Teacher's Sourcebook.* Ed. Gary Tate and Edward Corbett. New York: Oxford University Press, 1981. 89–99.

Knoblauch, C. H., and Lil Brannon. "Teacher Commentary on Student Writing: The State of the Art." *Rhetoric and Composition.* Ed. Richard L. Graves. Upper Montclair, NJ: Boynton/Cook, 1984. 285–291.

Lado, Robert. "Excerpts from 'Linguistic across Cultures.'" *Language Transfer in Language Learning.* Ed. Susan Gass and Larry Selinker. London: Newbury House, 1983. 21–32.

Lauer, Janice M., and William J. Asher. *Composition Research: Empirical Designes.* New York: Oxford University Press, 1988.

Lawson, Bruce, Susan S. Ryan, and W. Ross Winterowd. *Encountering Student Texts: Interpretive Issues in Reading Student Writing.* Urbana, IL: National Council of Teachers of English, 1989.

Lindemann, Erika. *A Rhetoric for Writing Teachers.* New York: Oxford University Press, 1982.

Liu, James J. Y. 1975. *Chinese Theories of Literature.* Chicago: University of Chicago Press, 1975.

Lu, Min-zhan. "From Silence to Words: Writing as Struggle." *College English* 49 (1987): 437–448.

Lukacs, Georg. *Essays on Realism.* Ed. Rodney Livingstone. Trans. David Fernbach. Cambridge: MIT Press.

Lynch, Denise. "Easing the Process: A Strategy for Evaluating Composition." *College Composition and Communication* 33 (1982): 310–314.

Maanen, John Van. *Tales of the Field: On Writing Ethnography.* Chicago: University of Chicago Press, 1988.

Mao, Tze-tung. "Talks at the Yenan Forum on Literature and Art." *Selected Works of Mao Tse-Tung,* vol. 4. London: Lawrence and Wishart Ltd, 1956. 63–93.

Marcus, George E., and Michael M. Fischer. *Anthropology as Cultural Critique.* Chicago: University of Chicago Press, 1986.

Milic, Louis T. "Theories of Style and Their Implications for the Teaching of Composition." *College Composition and Communication* 16 (1965): 66–69.

Myer, Miles. *A Procedure for Writing Assessment and Holistic Scoring.* Urbana, IL: ERIC Clearinghouse on Reading and Communication Skills and the National Council of Teachers of English, 1980.

Newkirk, Thomas. "How Students Read Student Essays: An Exploratory Study." *Written Communication* 1 (1984): 283–305.

———, ed. *Only Connect: Uniting Reading and Writing.* Upper Montclair, NJ: Boynton/Cook, 1986.

———, ed. *To Compose: Teaching Writing in High School and College.* 2nd ed. Portsmouth, NH: Heinemann, 1990.

Nochlin, Linda. *Realism: Style and Civilization.* New York: Viking Penguin, 1971.

North, Stephen M. *The Making of Knowledge in Composition: Portrait of an Emerging Field.* Upper Montclair, NJ: Boynton/Cook, 1987.

Ohmann, Richard. "Use Definite, Specific, Concrete Language." *The Writing Teacher's Sourcebook.* Ed. Gary Tate and Edward Corbett. New York: Oxford University Press, 1982. 379–389.

Plato. *Phaedrus and the Seventh and Eighth Letters.* Trans. Walter Hamilton. New York: Penguin, 1973.

Purves, Alan C. "In Search of an Internationally Valid Scheme for Scoring Compostions." *College Composition and Communication* 5 (1984): 426–438.

———. "The Teachers as Reader: An anatomy." *College English* 46 (1984): 259–265.

———, ed. *Writing Across Languages and Cultures: Issues in Contrastive Rhetoric.* Ann Arbor, MI: BKS Demand, 1988.

———. "Clothing the Emperor: Towards a Framework Relating Function and Form in Literacy." *Journal of Basic Writing* 10 (1991): 33–50.

Raymond, James. "What We Don't Know about the Evaluation of Writing." *College Composition and Communication* 33 (1982): 450–452.

Ridley, Charles Price. *Educational Theory and Practice in Late Imperial China: The Teaching of Writing as a Specific Case.* Ann Arbor, MI: University Microfilms International, 1980.

Schuster, Charles, ed. *The Politics of Writing Instruction: Postsecondary.* Portsmouth, NH: Boynton/Cook, 1991.

Schwartz, Mimi. "Response to Writing: A College-wide Perspective." *College English* 46 (1984): 55–62.

Searle, Dennis, and David Dillon. "The Message of Marking: Teacher Written Responses to Student Writing at Intermediate Grade Levels." *Research in the Teaching of English,* 14 (1980): 233–242.

Shen, Fan. "The Classroom and the Wider Culture: Identity as a Key to Learning English Composition." *College Composition and Communication* 40 (1989): 459–466.

Siegel, Muffy E. A. "Responding to Student Writing." *College Composition and Communication* 33 (1982): 302–309.

Sommers, Nancy. "Responding to Student Writing." *College Composition and Communication* 33 (1982): 148–156.

Sontag, Susan. *Against Interpretation.* New York: Farrar Straus Giroux, 1964.

Tobin, Joseph J. "A Visual Anthropology and Multivocal Ethnography: A Dialogical Approach To Japanese Preschool Class Size." *Dialectical Anthroplogy* 13 (1989): 173–187.

Tobin, Joseph J, David Y. H. Wu, and Dana H. Davidson. *Preschool in Three Cultures.* New Haven: Yale University Press, 1989.

Tocqueville, Alexis de. *Democracy in America.* New York: Vintage, 1945.

Tompkins, Jane. *Sensational Designs: The Cultural Work of American Fiction 1790-1860.* New York: Oxford University Press, 1985.

Warehime, Nancy. *To Be One of Us: Cultural Conflict, Creative Democracy, and Education.* Albany: State University of New York Press, 1993.

White, Edward M. "Post-Structural Literary Criticism and the Response to Student Writing." *College Composition and Communication* 35 (1984): 186–195.

———. ed. *Teaching and Assessing Writing.* San Francisco: Jossey-Bass, 1985.

Zamel, Vivian. "Responding to Student Writing." *TESOL Quarterly* 19 (1985): 79–101.

Zhou, Wei, ed. *Traditional Theories on Writing* (in Chinese). Xuchang, Henan: Wenxin Publishing House, 1989.

INDEX

Agnosticism, 114
Ahistoricism, 120
Ambiguity, 50, 51
Ambivalence, 81, 83, 89, 94
Analects of Confucius (Confucius), 115
Antiromanticism, 124
Aristotle, 119
Atmospherics, 79, 80, 87, 89
Authority, x, 42, 44, 88, 91, 115, 120

Bai Juyi, 34, 130*n9*
Balzac, Honoré, 13
"Beat Them 'Til They're Black and
  Blue," 27–29, 48–50, 98*tab,* 99–102,
  113–114
The Book of Odes (Confucius), 87, 131*n11*

Catharsis, 78
Characterization, 70, 87, 100
Chekhov, Anton, 13
Cliches, 39–40, 66, 80, 85, 108
Communication, 2, 26; and language, 65;
  writing as, 75
Composition, 4, 73
Confucius, ix, 14, 15, 95, 115, 116, 117,
  125
Conservatism, 24, 88, 89, 90
Content, xi
Contests, composition, 20, 97
Contrivance, 47, 69, 70, 74–77, 91, 92,
  104
Cooper, Charles, 128
Creativity, 74, 116
Credibility, 118
Cultural: bias, 127; critiques, 9; differ-
  ences, vii, 5, 111–112; divisions, 90;

forces, 2; pluralism, xiii, 88; truth in,
  xiii
Cultural Revolution, ix, x, 15, 16, 34,
  115, 129*n2*
Cynicism, 17, 57, 76

Davidson, Dana, 4
Decision-making, 78, 80, 113
Deng Xiaoping, x
Dickens, Charles, 13, 26
Diederich, Paul, 1
Dramatization, 81
Dream of the Red Chamber (Tsao Hsueh-
  chin), 66, 121, 131*n8*
Du Fu, 34, 76, 130*n2,* 130*n5,* 130*n8*

Eliot, T.S., 123, 124
Emotion, 16, 54, 55, 56, 60, 90, 108, 110,
  122, 126; expressing, 57
Empiricism, 120
Ethnography, multivocal, 4–6
Exams, entrance, 15, 20, 33, 58. *See also*
  Imperial Exam
Existence, 82
Experimentation, 39–40
Expression, 88; of emotion, 55, 57; fresh-
  ness of, 63; individuality of, viii, 34;
  means of, 77–80; self, 34, 91, 101, 126

Fan Shen, 127, 128
Faulkner, William, 27, 39–40
Feedback, 2
Feelings, confronting, 43
Feng You-lan, 123
Form, xi, 47, 70, 93, 127; basic, 73; natu-
  ral, 46; teaching, 73, 74; traditional,
  72–74